LINCOLN CHRISTIAN COLLEGE AND SEMINARY

BEYOND MAINTENANCE TO MISSION

BEYOND MAINTENANCE TO MISSION

A THEOLOGY OF THE CONGREGATION

Craig L. Nessan

Minneapolis   Fortress Press

BEYOND MAINTENANCE TO MISSION:
A Theology of the Congregation

Copyright © 1999 Augsburg Fortress. All rights reserved. Except for brief quotations in critical articles or reviews, no part of this book may be reproduced in any manner without prior written permission from the publisher. Write to: Permissions, Augsburg Fortress, P.O. Box 1209, Minneapolis, MN 55440.

Scripture quotations from the Revised Standard Version of the Bible are copyright © 1946, 1952, 1971 by the Division of Christian Education of the National Council of the Churches of Christ in the U.S.A. and are used by permission.

Scripture quotations from the New Revised Standard Version of the Bible are copyright © 1989 by the Division of Christian Education of the National Council of the Churches of Christ in the U.S.A. and are used by permission.

Cover design: Brad Norr Design
Interior design: Beth Wright

Library of Congress Cataloging-in-Publication Data

Nessan, Craig L.
    Beyond maintenance to mission : a theology of the congregation / Craig L. Nessan.
        p.   cm.
    Includes bibliographical references.
    ISBN 0-8006-3152-8 (alk. paper)
    1. Mission of the church. I. Title.
    BV601.8.N37 1999   98-48889
    250—dc21   CIP

The paper used in this publication meets the minimum requirements of American National Standard for Information Sciences–Permanence of Paper for Printed Library Materials, ANSI Z329.48-1984.

Manufactured in the U.S.A.   AF 1-3152
03   02   01   00   2   3   4   5   6   7   8   9   10

CONTENTS

99831

PART THREE: MISSION

PREFACE

The title of a recent book by Wendell Berry asks the basic but penetrating question: *"What are people for?"* By posing this fundamental query, Berry intends to probe the misdirection of farm policy in the United States since World War II. The operating assumption, that there are too many people working in agriculture, has shredded the fabric of rural life.

This book poses an equally basic and penetrating question regarding church life in the United States at the close of the twentieth century: *"What are congregations for?"* It may be that we have grown so accustomed to the routine of congregational life that we have stopped asking this question. Relying on established patterns, we delude ourselves into believing we are providing clear theological vision and faithful leadership. Thus we succumb to what Karl Hommen refers to as "the peril of ordinary days." Although there may be security in treading familiar roads, the situation in which the church finds itself at the dawn of a new century calls for a renewal of vision about how *God* seeks to engage Christian congregations. When congregational leaders cease struggling with this question—the question of God's purposes for the local congregation—a myriad of other priorities arise to divert us from this most central concern.

Congregations exist for the sake of mission. This fundamental truth about the church is easily set aside in favor of what appear to be more urgent agendas. Chief among these in this age of diminishing resources is the challenge of institutional survival. The "mission" of a congregation may eventually shrink to preoccupation with holding worship services and paying the bills. On other fronts, the vitality of congregational mission is narrowed by exaggerated emphasis on statistical growth, entertainment-style worship, or overly therapeutic models of ministry.

This book is written for congregational leaders, pastors, seminarians, and others in the church as a way of thinking systematically about the nature and purpose of the Christian congregation. It is an exercise in the art of "contextual theology," taking as our primary context the reality of congregational life as it has come to expression in North American experience. While we have much to learn from the varied expressions of church life in other parts of the world (for example, the basic ecclesial communities of Latin America), the shape of the church in North America remains the familiar institution of the local congregation.

The thesis of this book is that Christian congregations are uniquely situated in North American society to serve as *"centers for mission"* that both minister to the needs of members and carry forth the gospel beyond themselves to their communities and world. To this end a model of congregational life is proposed by which to examine how we can respond faithfully to God's calling. In order to maintain our focus on mission, we need to think carefully about what we are doing, both in terms of theology and praxis. This work aims to balance both of these emphases, allowing theology and praxis to inform one another mutually.

The "theology of the congregation" here articulated revolves around two central foci: *identity* and *mission*. Neither focus may be omitted without distorting what I believe to be the congregation's divine calling. Under the rubric of *identity,* we will consider the centrality of worship, education, fellowship, and stewardship in forming a congregation's proper self-understanding. Under the category of *mission,* attention shifts to evangelism, global connections, ecumenism, and social ministry. One unique feature about this theological approach is the prominence of *worship* in providing orientation for everything a congregation is and does. The historic elements and structure of Christian liturgy continue to offer the church direction for reestablishing the vitality of congregational life, if only we can devote to these ancient rituals the creativity and imagination they deserve.

I wish to express my deepest gratitude to: James W. Erdman for serving as my dialogue companion, constructive critic, and friend throughout the course of this project; Norma Cook Everist for her partnership in teaching these themes and especially for her commitment to the ministry of all the baptized; Rebecca Bauman for her ready and capable cooperation in a multitude of tasks; LaDonna Ekern and David Frerichs for their help as my student assistants; Judy Schroeder for first proposing Diagram 2 in chapter one; the entire faculty and staff of Wartburg Theological Seminary for their collegial support and passion for learning that leads to mission; and the seminary students from whom I learn every day. I wish also to acknowledge my love and appreciation for the members of my family who serve as my base of support in this and every endeavor: Cathy, Ben, Nate, Sarah, Andrew, Jessica, and Mary Catherine.

This book is dedicated to the saints of Trinity Evangelical Lutheran Church in Philadelphia, Pennsylvania, and St. Mark Lutheran Church in Cape Girardeau, Missouri, where I have served as pastor. From these members of Christ's church—militant and triumphant—I have learned the joy of pastoral ministry and the responsibility of clearly articulating a vision of Christian mission.

Christ the King
Dubuque, Iowa
1998

PART ONE

ORIENTATION

ONE

BASIC ELEMENTS OF A
THEOLOGY OF THE CONGREGATION

Everyone has one. Most often it remains invisible until an argument has broken out. "We can't have communion every Sunday." "What will the neighbors say if we start sheltering homeless people in the church basement?" "Let's budget more this year for janitorial service and take the difference out of our benevolence giving." One's theology of the congregation shapes in a million ways how one sets priorities for the work of the church.

Put most basically, one's theology of the congregation is evidenced by how one understands God to be present and working in everything a congregation chooses to do. Most often one's theology of the congregation remains implicit and therefore unexamined. That is the way we often look at institutions we think we already know (for example, marriage). Yet failure to reflect carefully upon the entire scope of ministry can leave a congregation ill-equipped to engage in the mission God sets before it.

In this initial chapter we establish the frame of reference for a comprehensive and vital theology of the congregation. The theology here developed stands in continuity with the early church, exists in a dynamic interplay between the issues of identity and mission, and is grounded in the historic liturgy of Word and Sacrament.

KERYGMA, KOINONIA, AND DIAKONIA

Three Greek words are frequently cited to express the identity of the earliest Christian church and its mission: *kerygma*, *koinonia*, and *diakonia*. Often they have been translated into English as proclamation, fellowship, and service, respectively. We will here preserve the Greek originals, with the intention of respecting the nuances of meaning lost in the translation.

The early church lived in acute tension with its surrounding cultures. When one reads accounts of the early Christian witnesses at the time the New Testament books conclude, for example, the letters of Ignatius or Polycarp, one is struck by the immediacy of persecution and martyrdom. Christians lived in an environment that was at best indifferent and that frequently organized acts of hostility against them. The main cause for their troubles was their peculiar confession of the Lordship of one Jesus Christ, crucified by the Romans, but for them the source of their own and the world's salvation. This confession of faith might have been excusable were it not for their persistence in seeking to spread these beliefs to others. What is more, the Lordship of Jesus over their lives made them suspect both among their Jewish neighbors and to the Roman authorities. A widening breach separated the early Christians from the Jewish communities that spawned them, as the confession of Jesus acted as a monumental stumbling block. This meant that the provisions for Jews under Roman law were insufficient to protect them. Furthermore, Christians who failed sufficiently to do obeisance to Caesar and demonstrate loyalty as Roman citizens became subject to persecution.

In this adverse climate, Christian believers organized life around three central concerns. The first of these, *kerygma,* refers not just to formal preaching but to proclamation of the Christian gospel in a variety of forms. By "gospel" these Christians meant the message of Jesus crucified and risen from the dead by which salvation from sin, evil powers, and death had been won. Those who put faith in Jesus and transferred allegiance to him formed a countercultural community, providing mutual edification and proclamation of the message so that others might join their ranks and be saved.

A central occasion for the *kerygma* was the assembly of believers for worship. Those appointed to preside over the Eucharist would also serve as interpreters of the readings from Holy Scripture. Where there were readings from the Hebrew Bible, emphasis was placed on fulfillment in Christ. Readings from Paul, the Gospels, and other New Testament writings also invited interpretation. Much of this proclamation took shape as exhortation and advice for persevering faithfully in the face of misunderstanding and opposition. A holy life could serve as a powerful witness to the truth of the Christian *kerygma.*

The *kerygma* was also extended by those doing the work of an evangelist. In addition to the testimony of the Christian faithful to family and neighbors, itinerant evangelists carried the gospel message far and wide. Paul provides a very early model of how the *kerygma* became known throughout and beyond the expanse of the Roman empire. Entering a city or town, Paul went first to the local synagogue and entered into debate about the meaning of the Jewish Bible in light of the coming of Jesus Christ. Where his message was received, Paul established a congregation for the nurture and spreading of the gospel. Where met by opposition, Paul took the gospel to the Gentile population and sought to build a local congregation. In either case, Gentiles were welcomed into the Christian community on the basis of confession of faith in the *kerygma* and baptism in the name of Christ.

What is difficult to recapture is the dynamic power intrinsic to early Christian announcement of the *kerygma*. The living Christ, clothed in human testimony, encountered hearers to set them free from fear and empowered them for a Christlike lifestyle in community with other believers. The message was not an abstraction about Jesus but rather a declaration of his living presence among them. Whether in personal testimony or in the public forum, the *kerygma* embodied the Christ and re-presented him as a living personality with whom one was invited to contend. Forgiveness of sins, deliverance from evil, and eternal life were gifts offered by Jesus Christ, too good to be true.

The second characteristic of the life of the early church is summarized by the term *koinonia*. The origin of Christian *koinonia* relies upon the initiative of God in establishing communion with humankind. The undeserved and gracious love of God *(agape)* entered the world in the incarnation of Jesus to create fellowship both with God and among humankind. Jesus gathered around himself a community of disciples, exemplified by the twelve. Jesus was renowned and even notorious for the fellowship he initiated—with sinners, tax collectors, lepers, Gentiles, women, and children. Particularly scandalous was Jesus' practice of open table fellowship. The kingdom of God meant for Jesus a community of egalitarian friendship under God's grace.

After Jesus' death and resurrection, *koinonia* with Jesus continued in the ritual eating and drinking of bread and wine known as the Eucharist. The Christian faithful continued to gather together, especially on the day of the resurrection (Sunday), to bless and break bread together in the name of Jesus. Through words of remembrance, prayers, and sacrament, Jesus lived among them bearing gifts of salvation. This *koinonia* with God in Jesus rests at the heart of all Christian fellowship.

Given the care of God in Christ for them, the early church lived also in mutual love and care for one another. The Acts of the Apostles reports that, "All who believed were together and had all things in common; they would sell their possessions and goods and distribute the proceeds to all, as any had need" (Acts 2:44–45). Special concern was demonstrated for widows and orphans within the community. The church recognized the value of its community life as a form of witness in demonstrating how Christians love one another. This testimony was seriously challenged when the church was forced to consider the entry of Gentiles into its fellowship. Did Gentiles first have to accept elements of the Jewish law and lifestyle before acceptance into Christian fellowship? Not without controversy, this debate was eventually settled by requiring nothing other than confession of faith and baptism.

The essence of Christian *koinonia* involves the quality of a community's life together. Does a community reflect the spirit of mutual love and concern shown by Jesus to those who followed him? Are all made welcome in the name of Jesus? Is the ultimate source of power that of the crucified Christ, and is that power shared in common? Is special effort made to express concern for the least of the sisters and brothers? And, when there is failure to live up to the ideal, is there readiness to ask for and grant forgiveness for Christ's sake? Each of these questions addresses aspects of Christian *koinonia* and are as validly asked of the quality of church life today as of ages past.

The final characteristic of early Christian community is *diakonia,* service. From this root we derive the term "deacon" which designates an office in the church committed to deeds of service to others. The model for all Christian service returns to the example of Jesus who defined human greatness not with images of wealth or authority but by the image of the servant kneeling down to wash dirty feet. Jesus' ultimate act of service entailed the sacrifice of his very own life on the cross as an expression of God's love, forgiveness, and salvation.

The *diakonia* of the early church was most evident in activities of healing, reconciling, and feeding. The brokenness of human life is nowhere more apparent than where people are sick, at odds, or hungry. The church carried forward Jesus' own ministry of healing by visiting the sick and anointing and praying for them. The needs of the grieving, widows and orphans, were likewise a portion of the healing work. The message of reconciliation was announced wherever conflict threatened to dismember the body of Christ. One thinks particularly of Paul's efforts at reconciliation in his correspondence with the Corinthian congregation. As often as the gospel was preached, the appeal was not only to be reconciled with God but also with one another. Feeding the hungry and needy was practiced by early Christians through programs of collection and distribution. These efforts stood in continuity with Jesus' own feeding miracles and the fourth petition of the Lord's prayer, "Give us this day our daily bread." Though early Christian communities were neither situated nor organized to enact structural change in society, especially given their convictions about the imminent parousia, there was a consistent pattern of selfless service to others that marks Christian *diakonia*.

Taken together, these three characteristics, *kerygma, koinonia,* and *diakonia,* typify Christian community from the very beginning. Each of these ancient functions will find elaboration in the theology of the congregation here developed.

FROM IDENTITY TO MISSION AND BACK AGAIN

Between the early generations of the Christian church and the present, some changes have taken place. No longer do we readily recognize the meanings of the three Greek terms, *kerygma, koinonia,* and *diakonia*. Between our time and theirs looms the monumental shift in Christian consciousness marked by Christianity's becoming the favored religion of the Roman empire during the fourth century. As baptism became requisite as a matter of citizenship, the level of individual commitment diminished. When everyone gets baptized, the meaning of baptism gets watered down. Today we employ different operating categories from those of the early church.

Nevertheless, Christ's commission to the church, to make disciples of all nations, remains as valid today as ever before. In order to carry out its mandate, the church must forever attend to two fundamental tasks: formation of Christian *identity* and faithfulness to the *mission* of the gospel. "Identity" is a modern concept strongly influenced by psychology. It refers to the foundational self-understanding of an individual. Applied to a group, identity is related to communal self-understanding.

The Christian contention is that individual identity finds its genuine expression only through confession of faith in Jesus as Lord as sacramentally enacted in baptism. The group identity of the church is commensurate with this, a community rooted in the way of Christ.

"Mission," the second task, refers to the purpose for which the church exists. Christian mission derives from the apostolic "sending out" of disciples by Jesus into the world to proclaim the gospel and extend the kingdom. Focus on identity without mission reduces the church to a social club whose only reason to exist is for the comfort and security of its membership. Focus on mission without the nurture of identity and the church begins to disintegrate into hyperactivity without direction. Identity without mission leads to self-absorption. Mission without identity leads to amnesia and exhaustion. Both must be related in dynamic interaction.

The model of congregational life here proposed dissects both identity and mission, each into four subcategories. The Christian congregation must attend to its *identity* by careful reflection on and execution of its (1) worship life, (2) teaching ministry, (3) fellowship, and (4) stewardship. Congregational *mission* entails conscientious efforts at (1) evangelism, (2) making global connections, (3) building ecumenical bridges, and (4) engagement in appropriate social ministry. Taken together, these components offer a comprehensive approach to congregational ministry. This does not mean every congregation will incorporate these elements in the same way. But moving from its current position, every congregation will benefit from employing these criteria to measure the wholeness of its ministry.

The model here proposed should be understood as a dynamic system. At one juncture in its life, a congregation may give priority to the focus on Christian identity by building up its efforts in the areas of worship, education, fellowship, and/or stewardship. Particular attention may have to be given to one or more of the four component aspects of identity formation. At other times (probably far more frequently), it is the mission of the congregation that requires added focus. Special attention will be directed toward a congregation's efforts in evangelism, global connections, ecumenism, or social ministry. At no time, however, ought the two central foci, identity and mission, be severed from one another. To do so is to jeopardize a congregation's health.

Larger congregations will find it possible, with their bigger membership and budgets, to address a greater number of these concerns simultaneously. Small congregations certainly need to think on a more modest scale but nonetheless can discover ways of enhancing each of the designated components. It is vital that local leaders begin by paying careful attention to the given congregational context with appreciation for the history and resources that are already in place.

What is exciting about this theology of the congregation is that the starting point for all else is the worship life of the congregation. Even in the most marginalized of congregations, worship remains a tremendous source of renewal as long as the baptized continue to gather together on Sundays. As shall be articulated in the pages that follow, all of the essential components of congregational life are already present in the historic Christian liturgy.

Diagram 1 summarizes the theology of the congregation to be elaborated in the remainder of this book. Again, the various components of the model need to be viewed in dynamic interrelationship one with the other.

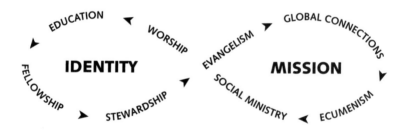

DIAGRAM 1

This chart demonstrates the various components of the model, centered around the two central foci of identity and mission. Congregations are challenged to evaluate their priorities by examining their ministries in all eight areas of congregational life.

One limitation of this depiction is that it lends the impression that ministry in each of the eight areas occurs in a linear sequence. Instead, the model seeks to demonstrate a lively interchange among all areas of congregational life, with special emphasis on the catalytic function of worship to revitalize all other aspects of congregational ministry. Another limitation is that the reader may be given the impression that the focus on congregational identity is something different from the focus on mission. Instead, the focus on identity must be viewed as integral to and serving the larger focus on congregational mission. As a corrective to these limitations, consider Diagram 2, which indicates the complexity of relationships among the various components of the model.

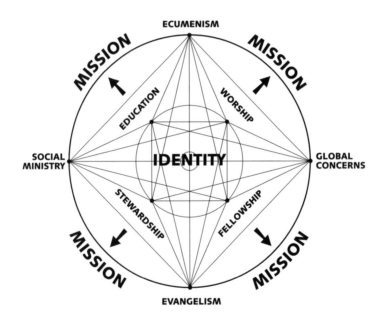

DIAGRAM 2

Each and every component exists in vital relationship with all of the others. The necessary focus on a congregation's identity is clearly in service of the larger Christian focus on mission.

GROUNDED IN LITURGY OF WORD AND SACRAMENT

Frequently one hears appeals for new forms and innovative styles of worship as necessary for church growth and renewal. In recent history, many have argued for alternative liturgies and worship as "entertainment evangelism." Especially at a time when the church is on retreat at several fronts, the temptation is strong to jettison the ballast of ancient liturgy in favor of what appear to be more accessible and attractive forms. This is not to argue against occasional experimentation in ritual. But this approach advocates instead for a fresh understanding of the historic liturgy as the single most important key for renewing congregational life and mission.

Although congregations week after week assemble for worship using a historic rite, little do they appreciate the treasure that has been preserved for them through the ages. The historic liturgy (properly known as the Roman rite) traces its origin back to the earliest centuries of Christianity. While there are today a plethora of churches advertising themselves as "Bible" churches, the entirety of the historic liturgy is founded on biblical material. Often the texts for worship (for example, in the confession of sins or the hymns of praise) are taken directly from Scripture. Regular use of the lectionary ensures that at least four Bible passages are read each Sunday. Sermons are based on texts from God's Word. The entire communion liturgy is constructed from biblical materials. There can be no more Bible-based worship than that which follows the historic liturgy.

The shape of the liturgy was developed over a number of centuries. Elements of the liturgy used today were already in place at the time of such Christian witnesses as Justin Martyr (c. 155) and Hippolytus (c. 200). The Roman rite, which contains virtually all the liturgical forms still in use today, was fixed already in the fifth century. When we worship using the historic liturgy, not only are we connected with Christians over the ages, but we are immersed in an encounter with God in Christ that has been effective in preserving the faith for nearly two thousand years!

At the time of the Reformation there were those, like Carlstadt and Zwingli, who were convinced that the reform of the church entailed the virtual abandonment of the Roman mass. Martin Luther, however, took a more conservative approach, revising the mass for the sake of a clearer proclamation of the gospel while preserving its essential structure and flow. Among the alterations implemented by Luther were the recovery of the sermon, introduction of hymns in the vernacular, emphasis on the Words of Institution within the communion liturgy, and participation of the people in the entire service, particularly as those who partake of the holy communion with Christ in bread and wine. Above all Luther was concerned to reform the notion of the mass as a sacrifice offered to God by the priest and replace it with belief in a gracious God who meets us in Christ as the center of worship.

Where liturgy remains vibrant, this conviction always abides: *God* is the primary actor in worship! This means that worship itself is sacramental in character; Christ meets us in Word and Sacrament and we are transformed. A congregation that places its trust in God's gracious presence in worship, Word and Sacrament, is establishing the foundation upon which the entirety of its ministry can develop and thrive. A congregation that underestimates the power of God in worship is in danger of losing not only its zeal for mission but its very soul.

An interpretation of worship is the thread that ties together this entire book. While there are numerous angles from which one can examine what happens in worship, for theological purposes it is vital to stress the pedagogical dimension of participating in worship. This does not mean turning the worship service into a lecture hall or Bible discussion group. Rather, one's very participation in the historic liturgy is itself an immersion in Christian reality that we need to articulate and reflect upon more intentionally in order to understand what is happening to us when we worship. Proper appreciation for the dramatic action of worship provides the basis for everything a congregation does in education, stewardship, evangelism, social ministry, and all else. The danger of this approach is that we undermine the mystery of glorifying God in worship through overanalysis. Yet, given the crisis of Christian catechesis and discipleship today, this approach seems imperative.

The early Christian church in its rites of initiation practiced what was called an "arcane discipline." This referred to the gradual revelation of Christian truth to converts in an extended catechetical process. The church led initiates step-by-step ever deeper into knowledge of Christian teaching. Initially inquirers to the faith were even dismissed from worship prior to the Eucharist liturgy. There remained ever

deeper mysteries of the faith to learn and explore. Outsiders to the
church had little awareness of or appreciation for the depths of Christian teaching. We would do well to recover a measure of arcane discipline in our approach to worship. Contrary to the prevalent notion
that the liturgy is repetitive and boring, there are treasures buried
here that the uninitiated cannot begin to discover. Contained in the
historic order of Christian worship is an agenda for congregational
ministry to last an eternity.

FOR FURTHER READING

Clapp, Rodney. *A Peculiar People: The Church as Culture in a Post-Christian
    Society.* Downers Grove: InterVarsity, 1996.

Cox, Harvey. *The Secular City: Secularization and Urbanization in Theological
    Perspective.* New York: Macmillan, 1966.

Dulles, Avery. *Models of the Church: A Critical Assessment of the Church in All Its
    Aspects.* Garden City, N.Y.: Doubleday & Co., 1974.

Hanover Report of the Anglican-Lutheran International Commission. *The
    Diaconate as Ecumenical Opportunity.* London: Anglican Communion Publi-
    cations, 1996.

Kung, Hans. *The Church.* New York: Sheed & Ward, 1967.

Mead, Loren B. *Transforming Congregations for the Future.* New York: The
    Alban Institute, 1994.

O'Meara, Thomas Franklin. *Theology of Ministry.* New York/Ramsey: Paulist,
    1983.

Russell, Keith A. *In Search of the Church: New Testament Images for Tomorrow's
    Congregations.* New York: The Alban Institute, 1994.

Schwarz, Hans. *The Christian Church: Biblical Origin, Historical Transformation,
    and Potential for the Future.* Minneapolis: Augsburg, 1982.

Whitehead, Evelyn Eaton, and Whitehead, James D. *Method in Ministry: The-
    ological Reflection and Christian Ministry.* Kansas City, Mo.: Sheed & Ward,
    1995.

Wind, James P. *American Congregations.* Two volumes. Chicago: University of
    Chicago Press, 1994.

TWO

FIRST LISTEN

If the greatest of all spiritual gifts is love, then one of the purest expressions of love is to listen. In the words of Paul Tillich, "the first duty of love is to listen." Children need it. Spouses need it. Friends need it. You need it. And the church needs it. Before one begins to lead a congregation, one should listen carefully to that congregation's story. This means listening carefully to the stories of individuals and families. But it also means listening to the story of the congregation itself. Each congregation has its own unique biography—stories of birth, adolescence, maturity, and age.

Our listening to one another is grounded in God's faithful listening to us. We trust that God is always faithful to listen to our prayers, whether they come in the form of private devotions or public intercessions at worship. The Psalms as the "prayer book of the Bible" (Bonhoeffer) instruct us that God does not discriminate among prayers according to their content. We are free to direct to God our deepest thoughts and emotions, even those of anger and vengeance. As God is patient in listening to our cries, so we in the church have the responsibility to listen to the inmost concerns shared with us by our neighbor.

In this chapter we first examine the value of listening to a congregation's story. We continue by situating the congregational story within the larger context of our culture. Finally we locate both congregation and culture in the largest story of all, the biblical story of God's love for humanity.

CONGREGATIONAL STORY

First impressions are not always correct. Before attempting to introduce significant change, a congregational leader honors a people by genuinely seeking to understand why things are the way they are. What is the extant "theology" of this congregation? How is this theology reflected in the particular beliefs and practices of this parish? Who are the primary articulators of the congregation's theology? Are there dissenting viewpoints? What are the latent convictions and hopes awaiting future expression?

If one wants to learn the theology of a particular place and people, one must set aside plenty of time for visiting. While this visiting can take place either formally in people's homes or informally around the church, attention needs to be paid not only to the concerns of individuals but to how people express their understanding of the collective life of the congregation itself. Furthermore, people need to be invited to answer questions about how they see God working in their church. Where has God been powerfully present for them? Where do they believe the congregation could more effectively manifest God's involvement? How do they hope God might employ this congregation in the future?

Not only is it essential to talk together about the role of a particular congregation in God's ministry, but listening also involves paying attention to how a congregation goes about the work of ministry. The style of worship, for example, says much about a congregation's belief in the nature and purposes of God. How a congregation conducts its meetings and makes decisions also is indicative of its operative theology. If there exists a written history of the congregation, this contains invaluable information about its self-understanding. A written history can be tested against the viewpoints of long-standing members of the congregation to check for accuracy as to whether this is the prevailing current of opinion about the past. Mission statements, annual reports, and budget priorities give added insight into a congregation's theology. One can even look to the wider community and ask members and leaders of other churches about the reputation of a given church as a steward of God's grace.

Shared effort to identify a given congregation's theology can assist members to begin asking the right questions about its identity and its mission. Basic elements of a congregation's theology are reflected in how it answers basic questions about the faith:

1. What is the nature of sin? Which are the most threatening sins?
2. With what images is Jesus best described?
3. What is the nature of the salvation Jesus brings?
4. What are the most important tasks of the church?
5. What is the gospel? How does one best communicate it today?
6. What importance should the sacraments have in the church?
7. What is the purpose of confirmation?
8. How involved should the church be in social issues?

9. What is the meaning of stewardship?

10. What do Christians hope for beyond death?

Implicit behind everything a congregation decides and does is a particular notion of God and God's dealings with people. There may be some significant discrepancies between what is professed and what is practiced. Congregations are no different from individuals in this regard.

Expert resources have been written and are available to assist the inquirer in the process of discerning the extant theology of a particular congregation. Much recent work on "local theologies" helps instruct how to listen carefully to what is being expressed through various media, not only in words but in practice. A family systems model may likewise do much to reveal the inner dynamics of a congregation's life. Preparing a congregational genotype can offer great insight.

In every case a congregation will be enhanced by deliberate examination of its theology. By asking the right questions about what a congregation has been, is presently, and hopes to be doing, the orientation shifts in the direction of mission. People are reminded that above all God has a mission and that Christian congregations are to place themselves in league with that mission as their very reason for existence.

CULTURAL STORY

Congregations do not exist in a vacuum but are situated inextricably in a culture. On a continent so vast as North America, in fact there are numerous cultural influences that impinge upon congregational life, some of these global, some regional, some local. In what follows, only the broadest strokes can be employed to paint a picture of "American" culture. Special reference will be made to the descriptions provided by Douglas John Hall and Tex Sample.

Douglas John Hall, in his book *Thinking the Faith,* analyzes the North American context according to seven characteristics: the end of the Constantinian era, religious pluralism, the theological impact of Auschwitz, Marxism and the revolution of the oppressed, the nuclear crisis, the rebellion of nature, and apocalyptic consciousness with the rise of religious simplism. These categories provide a large scale framework for commenting on the global context in which North American congregations operate.

The end of the Constantinian era for the church and the impact of religious pluralism go hand in hand. Since the fourth Christian century, the church in the West has enjoyed the luxury of having Christianity as the implicit, and often explicit, religion of the culture. In the United States, although there has existed a legal separation of church and state, churches have been expected to provide religious sanction to affairs of state and have in turn received preferential status. Robert Bellah, among others, has analyzed the shape of an American civil religion that undergirds political life and in many instances blends indistinguishably into congregational belief and practice. Only recently has the church's position in society begun to erode with the emergence of multiform religious currents. Increasingly, Christianity finds itself as merely one religious option among many others. Its favored status has been challenged not only by a variety of religious competitors but also by the questionable value of religion itself in the eyes of many pragmatic Americans. Not without reason have intellectuals heralded the dawning of a new era in the West, adorning it with the name "post-Christian."

The specter of Auschwitz continues to haunt the Christian church. The failure of the church to stand up to the moral and political challenge of Jewish genocide raises profound questions about moral fiber. Christians failed not only by looking the other way but by active complicity in the arrest and execution of Jews. Is the church inherently anti-Semitic? The rise of new forms of anti-Jewish religion (e.g., Christian Identity) in the heartland of the United States demonstrates that the church must continue to articulate its mission in a way that honors Judaism. In North America this raises the subsequent question of the church's integrity in the face of radical evil as it continues to become manifest in world affairs.

With the fall of the Berlin wall in 1989, the fear of both Marxism and the nuclear peril have begun to subside in American consciousness. What does abide, however, is both the reality of the world's poor majority and the threat of nuclear weapons use, not necessarily by a world superpower but more probably in a regional conflict. Whereas the aspirations of the poor were previously dismissed under the suspicion of Communist agitation, the disparity between rich and poor can be viewed more clearly in a world devoid of the polarization created by the Cold War. The cries of the hungry continue to summon our attention and clamor for redress. Regarding the nuclear threat, while Americans sense relief at the relaxation of tension between the United States and the former Soviet Union, nuclear proliferation continues to undermine global security. The need for negotiation of nuclear weapons treaties is as urgent now as ever before.

Concern for the natural environment grows in the awareness of many Americans. Not only the importance of recycling but the dilemmas of resource depletion and waste disposal require priority on the church's agenda unprecedented in previous generations. Human beings are increasingly challenged to see themselves not above but within the complex web which we call the ecosystem. Human flourishing can no longer take place at the expense of the natural world, but rather human beings must understand themselves as part of the natural world, the part exclusively responsible for the present disequilibrium.

Finally, there is the strong temptation in an immensely complex world to reduce issues to a simple formula. Religious people are thus tempted to take refuge in an apocalyptic outlook that sees the only possible resolution to contemporary crises in the dramatic intervention of God in human history to punish the guilty and reward the faithful. Security is sought in authorities, whether Scripture or charismatic leaders, which are believed to shelter the faithful from the corruption of the decaying order. The consequences of such an approach are twofold: defense of the status quo lest any further erosion take place and passivity in addressing the imperatives of the future.

If Hall provides the contours for situating North America in the global context, Tex Sample, in his book *U.S. Lifestyles and Mainline Churches,* provides a guide for understanding some of the more subtle dynamics of American culture. Sample's analysis of American society is helpful in that he distinguishes between a "cultural left," a "cultural right," and a "cultural middle." Each of these groupings are further subdivided and characterized.

The cultural left is notable for the self-directedness of its ambitions, its relative affluence, and the value it places on personal choice and tolerance. Rejecting the perceived conformism of previous generations, the cultural left establishes its own priorities and agendas with wariness toward external authority. Benefiting from the affluence of the previous generation, however, the cultural left has acquired formidable educational credentials, which secure its own economic status.

Extraordinarily high value is placed upon freedom of choice in all matters of lifestyle, including religious preference. The only trait not tolerated is intolerance itself.

The cultural left can itself be divided into three subgroups: the "I-am-mes," the "Experientials," and the "Societally Conscious." The "I-am-mes" operate with a decided preference for novelty in their self-expression and tend to be the cultural left's youngest members. The "Experientials" focus on their own participation in unique life-experience, whether it be of the natural world, chemically-induced, or mystical. The "Societally Conscious" are at the forefront of movements for social and political change. Environmental activism, social justice advocacy, and world peace are major concerns. Within the purview of the cultural left falls also the New Age movement, with its interest in a holistic approach to self, others, society, nature, and the divine.

The cultural right, by contrast, is characterized by concern for providing life's basic necessities and by rootedness in a specific locale. Due to their economic status, members of the cultural right devote the major portion of their lives to securing food, shelter, and whatever niceties can be afforded. The most cherished value is what contributes to the well-being of the family. An ethos of the local community and neighborhood prevails, providing the parameters for this worldview.

The cultural right can also be subdivided into three categories: the "Respectables," the "Hard Living," and the "Desperate Poor." The "Respectables" constitute the largest portion of the cultural right. While occupational, and thus economic, advancement is limited by education and training, this group places great emphasis on leading a decent and respectable life within the given parameters. Of all the subdivisions of American culture, this one is the largest, consisting of 60 million Americans, who are undoubtedly the backbone of most Christian congregations.

The "Hard Living" consist of those hardy individuals whose lifestyles entail heavy labor and often heavy drinking. This group tends to live for today without concern for the morrow. There prevails an overriding sense of powerlessness, which translates all too often into marital strife and domestic violence. The "Desperate Poor" include both those locked in vicious cycles of intergenerational poverty and those who through age or misfortune can insufficiently provide for themselves.

The cultural right adheres to popular forms of religion and conventional morality. God's providence shapes the course of daily events. There is tremendous respect and authority lent to mediators of religious truth, both clergy and Scripture. Churches offer a strong sense of community that reinforces the prevailing orientation to the local setting. Personal devotion, expressed through confidence in the power of prayer to solve problems and the comfort of religious objects, is common. Going to church and loving one's country are integral to a respectable life.

The cultural middle places career at the center of existence. Successful members of this group have completed higher education and find themselves situated in jobs that offer a high level of satisfaction. In order to maximize their achievements in career, this group is typically mobile and places relatively little value on place or community. They are of necessity individualists who are frequently willing to postpone gratification to a later time in order to excel in their work. Spouses and families, while providing a base of support, must also be willing to make sacrifices for the sake of career advancement.

Again, the cultural middle can be divided into three subcategories: the "Successful," the "Strivers," and the "Conflicted." The "Successful" are those who are living out the American dream. Happy in their work, well-compensated, and able to afford the good things money can buy, this subgroup consists of the business executives, lawyers, physicians, politicians, and others who set the standards for "the good life." The "Strivers" aspire to the lifestyle of the "Successful," but, lacking either the opportunity or the skills, never quite make the grade. This subgroup, often leveling out in mid-management positions, nevertheless attempts to keep up with the upper echelon and often falls into serious debt in the process.

The third subcategory belongs to the "Conflicted," those caught between aspirations of career and commitment to their families. These do not fully share the willingness to sacrifice family stability for the sake of career achievement. At the same time, they are not ready to settle down in a lifestyle of respectability without affluence. However, their career paths do not make it likely they will ever ascend toward a higher standard of living. They are indeed caught in an irreconcilable conflict of values, leading to much frustration.

The religious leanings of the cultural middle are toward beliefs and practices that reinforce and provide legitimation for their position in society. Faith finds its proper orbit circling the personal needs of the individual. Success in career tends to be interpreted as a sign of God's blessing. Insofar as the corporate dimension is important, the church serves to support the individual's immediate family and provide an interesting array of study opportunities. The cultural middle places strong reservations on the role of the church in initiating social change. Ministering to the needs of the destitute is appropriate but not by advocating structural change. Members of the cultural middle are likely to hold positions of leadership in the church where their management and organization skills can be put to good use.

Sample's breakdown of American culture into a left, right, and middle provides a helpful tool for considering the theology of a particular congregation. Each congregation consists of its own peculiar mix of cultural styles. Depending on the constituency, the theological outlook will vary. This means that leadership in a particular parish will need to take seriously both the proclivities and weaknesses of the cultural persuasions of its members as it broadens its theological vision. To fail to reckon with prevailing attitudes will mean working at a disadvantage, if not dooming one to unproductive conflict. While the pages that follow propose a particular model of theology of the congregation, the proposed ideas will always require adaptation to meet local circumstances.

Neither Hall's account nor Sample's touches on every aspect of American culture. For example, the ubiquity of media in shaping popular opinion has hardly been mentioned. Consumerism remains a major competitor with religion for ultimate allegiance. Likewise the shift toward the service sector in the American economy and the problems of under- and unemployment have only been indirectly addressed by means of Sample's categories. The reader is invited to bring to this discussion his or her own cultural critique as it contributes to a fuller understanding of the context in which the local congregation does ministry.

BIBLICAL STORY

The story of a congregation does not begin with its local history nor end with its placement in a particular culture. Instead, the story of every Christian congregation begins with God's first Word spoken at creation and ends with the consummation of all things in God's eternity. It is vital that a congregation see itself in the perspective of God's own story, lest it stray from its God-given identity and mission.

This story begins with the wisdom of a God who freely decided to create a universe, including creatures to whom God entrusted a mind of their own. These creatures, humankind, although made for a unique relationship with God (made in God's very own image), are responsible for repeated and wanton rebellion against their maker. In choosing to follow after other gods, they lose not only the source of their very life but their own peace of mind. As a consequence, their relationships with others become severely troubled, even to the point of murder and war.

God, being compassionate and merciful, does not abandon humanity to its own self-destruction. Instead, God sends messenger after messenger with warning of ruin, should they continue on their current path, and with promise of grace, even when they fail to heed the warning. Abraham and Sarah, Moses and Miriam, Deborah and Isaiah, together with Ezra and Esther, each have left testimony to God's faithfulness. The people of Israel are God's chosen ones for bringing God's teachings and God's mercy to the entire world.

Long had a Messiah been anticipated who would usher in God's perfect kingdom of justice and peace. In the fullness of time, God sent a son into the world, born of Mary, to incarnate divine truth. Jesus preached and taught God's kingdom. God is not distant but near. God is not severe but merciful. In terse and captivating stories, Jesus revealed the nature of God's presence in the world. The sick were healed by his touch. Disciples were called into community. Sinners, forgiven, were welcomed home. The distinction between righteous and unrighteous, clean and unclean, insider and outsider, Jew and Gentile was erased in table fellowship with Jesus. The love he demonstrated broke all rules of propriety and threatened to disrupt the social order. Jesus died on the cross and was raised to new life on Easter. Doubting disciples heard, saw, and believed. God has chosen Jesus' death to inaugurate an age in which all people would hear the gospel that their sins are forgiven and that after death there awaits resurrection. All these gifts are ours for Jesus' sake.

God gave the Holy Spirit to the church that it might follow the way of Jesus and proclaim the gospel of forgiveness and love to all. For nearly two thousand years the church has struggled with this calling. At times the church has been willing to sacrifice much, even life itself, for the cause of Jesus. At other times the church has virtually forgotten its identity and mission. The history of the church—the age of the martyrs, the triumph of Christendom, the witness of reformers, and the challenge of the modern world—provides much seed for thought and practice as the church continues to search for orientation today.

The Christian congregation, whose building is located on a particular street corner or highway and whose members are influenced by the rapid currents of American culture, must see itself in the fuller perspective of God's dealings with humanity through Israel, Jesus, and the history of the church. The mission entrusted to the people of God of old belongs also to the church today and thereby to every congregation.

We are to be that people who name ourselves with the name of Jesus. Our identity is that of those for whom Jesus died. We are to gather together to worship and learn and befriend one another for the purpose of remembering Jesus. For Jesus' sake we are forgiven and have the hope of eternal life.

Equally, we are people with a purpose. Our mission is to share the good news by which we ourselves are identified. By word of mouth we tell others about the treasure that is ours in Christ. We invite them to come into our midst in the Christian congregation. We seek to build bridges with other Christian people from whom we are estranged. And we seek to link our lives ever more intentionally with Christian people across the globe. All of this we do in order that the gospel of Christ might be believed and the kingdom Jesus proclaimed might be present. Where governments, corporations, armies, or other powers contradict the rule of Christ, there the church summons its wisdom and courage to respond faithfully.

While as leaders in the church we begin by listening to the theology of the local congregation and pay attention to the strictures of the culture in which it finds itself, we must also remain steadfast to God's own story as it has unfolded over the ages. We must claim this story ever anew as our own heritage. If we fail to know our true identity and respond to our God-given mission, the cause is lost.

FOR FURTHER READING

Bellah, Robert N., and Neally, Robert. *Habits of the Heart: Individualism and Commitment in American Life.* Berkeley, Calif.: University of California Press, 1985.

Bevans, Stephen B. *Models of Contextual Theology.* Maryknoll: Orbis, 1992.

Eberle, Gary. *The Geography of Nowhere: Finding One's Self in the Postmodern World.* Kansas City, Mo.: Sheed & Ward, 1994.

Gergen, Kenneth J. *Saturated Self: Dilemmas of Identity in Contemporary Life.* San Francisco/New York: HarperCollins, 1991.

Hall, Douglas John. *Thinking the Faith, Professing the Faith, Confessing the Faith: Christian Theology in a North American Context.* Minneapolis: Fortress, 1989–96.

Hopewell, James F. *Congregation: Stories and Structures.* Philadelphia: Fortress, 1987.

Postman, Neil. *Amusing Ourselves to Death: Public Discourse in the Age of Show Business.* New York: Penguin Books, 1986.

Sample, Tex. *U.S. Lifestyles and Mainline Churches: A Key to Reaching People in the 90's.* Louisville: Westminster/John Knox, 1990.

Schreiter, Robert. *Constructing Local Theologies.* Maryknoll: Orbis, 1985.

Wuthnow, Robert. *Rediscovering the Sacred: Perspectives on Religion in Contemporary Society.* Grand Rapids: Eerdmans, 1992.

THREE

TRINITARIAN FOUNDATION

A trinitarian foundation undergirds this theology of the congregation. First, we pay attention to the God whose rule Jesus proclaimed at the heart of his message. We seek to reinvigorate congregational self-understanding with reference to the language of Jesus and the symbol of the kingdom of God. One of the most exciting trends in New Testament study is the rediscovery of what Jesus meant by the kingdom. The language Jesus used to describe God and God's activity, especially in his parables, informs our understanding of God's continuing involvement in the world today. Jesus' understanding of the kingdom reminds us that God is near and God is merciful. The wisdom of this God is a subversive wisdom.

Second, with reference to Christology, we draw upon Luther's insistence upon the real presence of Christ in Word and Sacrament. It is the crucified and risen Jesus Christ who is still alive to meet us when we gather together in worship for the sake of the gospel. Only as we trust that Christ is as alive among us as he was alive in earlier generations do we recognize the vital importance of what we do as Christian congregations.

Third, with regard to the Holy Spirit, we refer to the inexorable movement, demonstrated especially clearly in the letters of Paul, from proclamation of the gospel to *parenesis,* that is, to a life lived in conformity to the way of Jesus Christ. While our justification is solely by grace through faith in Christ, the Holy Spirit continues to enliven the church with gifts freshly incarnated in the lives of believers. Together the members of a congregation are the body of Christ in a certain time and place. The gospel sets us free for a life lived "in Christ."

After developing this trinitarian foundation, we begin in the next chapter with the theme of worship in building a theology that can serve both the identity and the mission of the congregation. Jesus Christ remains the cornerstone for the entire structure.

JESUS AND THE KINGDOM OF GOD

Jesus spoke of God's interaction with humankind in terms of "the kingdom." Both his aphorisms and his parables testify to a profound faith in the nearness and mercy of God given characteristic expression by this symbol. Today there are those who hesitate to employ the term "kingdom" out of fear that it is inseparable from an antiquated or oppressive social system. Those so inclined may take comfort in an alternative translation of *basileá toũ theoũ*: rule of God, commonwealth of God, fellowship of God, or even friendship of God. I will continue to employ the more literal translation, kingdom of God, precisely because what Jesus means by kingdom inverts the standards of success and power commonly regnant in human affairs.

Kingdom does not refer to a locale in time or space but to a particular mode of God's activity. While the full arrival of God's kingdom awaits future consummation, what is daring about Jesus' teachings is the claim that the kingdom already impinges upon the present, indeed is the single most important reality determining human life. The kingdom is present as Jesus casts out demons (Lk 11:20). The arrival of the kingdom is not measured by calculating signs but is already "in the midst of you" (Lk 17:20-21). The kingdom suffers violence at the hands of those who would seize it by force (Mt 11:12).

The teachings of Jesus, particularly his parables, demonstrate that where God rules, there is a dramatic reversal of expectations and values. Like the one discovering buried treasure in a field, the one discovering the kingdom acquires immeasurable joy (Mt 13:44). The kingdom lacks all sense of measure in apportioning forgiveness (Lk 15:11-32, Prodigal Son). There is an urgency to the affairs of the kingdom that requires leaving other matters behind (Mt 22:1-14, the Great Supper). Fairness yields to mercy in the kingdom (Mt 20:1-16, Laborers in the Vineyard). Mercy draws near from an impossible source (Lk 10:29-37, Good Samaritan). God is the source of mercy that surpasses any human example (Lk 18:1-8, the Unjust Judge). The increase of the kingdom, though mysterious, is guaranteed through the power of God (Mk 4:3-9, the Sower).

Though these summations of the parables are far too brief, they serve to underscore the nature of the kingdom that Jesus announced. Furthermore, the life of Jesus depicts action fully consistent with the view of the kingdom articulated in the parables. In the kingdom, all are welcome: children, women, unclean lepers, the demon-possessed, Gentiles, tax collectors, and public sinners. In the kingdom, the hungry are fed. Nowhere were the values of the kingdom more evident than in the table fellowship of Jesus. Disciple and opponent alike looked askance at the company Jesus not only kept but invited. It is fitting that it was in such table fellowship the night before his death that Jesus instituted a meal for his remembrance. Even from the cross Jesus testified to the mercy of the kingdom, inviting into paradise a penitent thief and praying forgiveness for those who executed him.

The kingdom of God that Jesus both taught and embodied revolves around two central convictions: God is near and God is merciful. God is not distant and detached from human affairs but near, involved, connected. The reality of the kingdom is "in, with, and under" the reality of the everyday, for those with the eyes to perceive. Jesus' life of prayer and his peculiar address for God as Abba—"Daddy," "Papa"—demonstrate a vivid sense of God's nearness and presence. At the same time this familiar term for God indicates Jesus' assurance that God is merciful. God is not severe and condemning, but invites and welcomes the sinner home. Jesus imparted this awareness of God's proximity and loving-kindness to his disciples as he taught them to pray and to live the Lord's Prayer: "Our Father...your kingdom come...forgive us our sins...as we forgive."

Marcus Borg in his book, *Jesus: A New Vision: Spirit, Culture, and the Life of Discipleship,* presents the case that the kingdom of God as proclaimed by Jesus runs counter to the precepts of conventional wisdom, now as well as then. Conventional wisdom operates with well-defined notions of family, wealth, honor, and religion. Family lines are carefully delineated; obligations of blood kinship have primacy; family structure is patriarchal. Wealth is a sign of God's favor, poverty a sign of divine absence or punishment. Honor comes to those with status and power over others; they command preferential treatment, especially when in the public eye. Religion is a matter of maintaining purity, that is, living a good life according to the prevailing mores.

The kingdom envisioned by Jesus contradicts each of the provisions of conventional wisdom. Regarding family, all are brothers and sisters under the parenthood of God in the kingdom. The community of Jesus is scandalously egalitarian. In the kingdom, true wealth consists of trust in God, not mammon. The least of the brothers and the sisters are the honored ones in the kingdom. The greatest must be the servants of all. Religion requires neither purity nor performance, but faith in the nearness and compassion of the living God in the kingdom. The wisdom of Jesus is subversive of conventional standards on all decisive points. Is it any wonder that this man's life ended in crucifixion?

The kingdom as proclaimed by Jesus was called into radical question by his death. The disciples scattered in fear. Jesus' enemies triumphed. Conventional wisdom prevailed, then as now. The rich get richer; the poor get poorer. The rest pay taxes to Caesar. All is right with the conventional world. Until Easter, that is. The resurrection of Jesus, however, means nothing is what it appears. The power of guilt to cripple is overcome by the forgiveness of sins granted by the superior power of the cross. The grip of evil—of Satan—is broken by the stronger grip of God's love. Even that which seems most certain of all, the reality of death, loses its control as God raised Jesus from the dead. With Jesus' resurrection, the promise is extended: all those who trust in Jesus, and thereby in the kingdom for which he stands, will share in his victory over sin, Satan, and death itself. Life in the kingdom, eternal life, is what lasts forever.

This construal of the life, teachings, death, and resurrection of Jesus, revolving around his vision of God's imminent and gracious kingdom, provides a first and essential point of reference for the theology of the congregation to follow. Keep in mind the kingdom!

LIVING WORD OF GOSPEL

Luther and the Reformers in the sixteenth century sought to recover a vivid awareness of the nearness of God to human life, the very incarnation of God in the human flesh of Jesus. In or out of the church, God's involvement means grace. In particular, the strictures of conventional religious wisdom, given expression at that time through a host of pious customs (not least the sale of certificates of pardon called indulgences), were forced to yield to Scripture's central message of God's love and grace revealed in the person of Jesus.

For Luther as for Paul, the nature of God's love was nowhere more profoundly, although paradoxically, revealed than in the wisdom of the cross. Luther clung to a theology of the cross over against all the theologies of glory that vie for human allegiance. It is not by our own merit or works, our own performance, that we attain God's favor. Solely for the sake of the sufferings of Jesus and by the grace of his resurrection do we dare hope for eternal life. All this is ours "by faith in the

Son of God who loved me and gave himself for me" (Luther's *Small Catechism*).

The central theological concern of the Reformation demonstrates striking congruity with Jesus' message of the kingdom. While focus definitely shifts from a Galilean's trusting response to the teaching of Jesus, to a German's faith in the person and works of Jesus, the content remains remarkably consistent. That content is summarized in a single word: *Gospel*. The good news preached by Jesus: The kingdom of God is at hand, nearby and gracious! The gospel according to the Reformers: Sins are forgiven and eternal life won by the death and resurrection of Christ! Both messages resound joyously in the ears and hearts of those estranged from God by virtue of their own guilt and fear. Both draw the believer near again to God, working reconciliation. Both liberate the captive, setting one free to love the neighbor.

The power of the gospel derives from the living presence of the crucified and risen Christ who comes to us in Word and Sacrament. Luther's theology differed from late medieval piety in its shift away from detached observance of religious rituals and customs, and toward an actual encounter with God in Christ. "Word" for Luther consisted not only of the reading of holy Scripture at worship, but especially of preaching, which becomes God's living Word for us today, convicting us of sin and recreating us by the power of Christ.

Regarding the sacraments, Luther was unshakable in his conviction that Christ is really present in the acts of Baptism and Holy Communion. God employs the commonest elements of the earth in service of the gospel—water, bread, wine—and attaches to them a living Word of promise. Just as God became incarnate in the flesh and blood of Jesus, so now Christ is actually present in the sacraments. Particularly in his dispute with Zwingli over the nature of Christ's presence in the bread and wine, Luther demonstrated a deep commitment to sacramental realism. Christ says the bread and wine are his body and blood, and so they are. The nature of Christ's presence, moreover, does not mean condemnation but forgiveness, grace, and new life, wrought by Christ himself.

This theology is wonderfully summarized in the seventh article of the Augsburg Confession concerning the church: "This is the assembly of all believers among whom the Gospel is preached in its purity and the holy sacraments are administered according to the Gospel." To risk a rough paraphrase, the church is where believers "have it done to them" by the gospel in preaching and sacraments. This means that God is the most important actor in what takes place in worship. It is this confessional conviction that is greatly at risk when we spurn a sacramental understanding of worship in favor of what is more appealing to consumers.

Permeating Luther's understanding of worship, preaching, and the sacraments is a vivid theology of the Holy Spirit. The Holy Spirit operates in fulfillment of God's promises as the Word of God is proclaimed and the sacraments are celebrated. By the power of the Holy Spirit, Christ is made present in the sacramental event. One can depend on Christ's presence because a special promise has been attached by God to these means of grace. Regin Prenter has described Luther's view as one of "dynamic realism." Christ is "really present" to accomplish God's work of redemption. This presence is "dynamic" insofar as Christ actually does something in the encounter. Sins are forgiven. Lives are changed. Eternal life is received.

All of the revisions in worship that Luther advocated in the sixteenth century were in service of an enhanced appreciation for the presence of Christ. Worship in the vernacular made it possible for worshipers to meet Christ in their own language. When the Word was preached, it was God who did the speaking, through the preacher. Congregational singing is an expression of gratitude not only for what God has done but for what God is continuing to accomplish among those assembled. People are to participate in Holy Communion, themselves receiving the sacrament in both kinds. Only so do they meet the living Christ, who bears gifts of salvation and whom they receive in faith.

Jesus' embodiment of the kingdom and Luther's defense of Christ's real and living presence in Word and Sacrament, taken together, provide a basis for rejuvenating the worship life of every Christian congregation. Yet, a third theological footing must be set. We turn next to a consideration of the movement from proclamation to *parenesis* in the letters of Paul.

FROM PROCLAMATION TO *PARENESIS*

Luther and the Reformers rightly insisted that justification is the central Christian doctrine by which the church stands or falls. Those confused about the central truth that we are made right with God by grace alone through faith alone have consciences that are burdened and lives that are driven by compulsions of various sorts. Luther grounded this brilliant theological insight on his reading of Paul's letter to the Romans. All have sinned and fall short of the glory of God. We are justified by Christ's death on the cross and receive God's declaration of forgiveness solely by faith. Baptism marks the death of the sinner and the raising up of the baptized as child of God. All of life is lived henceforth under the influence of Christ, that is, "in Christ."

Wherever one begins in reading Paul—with his letter to the Romans, the theology of the cross in First Corinthians, or with another text—the thrust of the Pauline epistles always moves toward instruction in the Christian life. Major portions of Paul's letters are devoted to a discussion of practices that raise challenges for Christian existence in the world. The exhortation and instruction for the Christian life found in the New Testament is called *parenesis* by scholars. While major attention has been focused on the doctrinal element in Paul's writings, the inexorable drive toward *parenesis* receives relatively scant comment. The parenetic element, however, provides some crucial direction for a theology of the congregation.

One must keep in mind that the communities that Paul instructed in his letters all gathered together regularly for worship. Within their own cultures, these Christian churches were suspected of scandal, followers of an odd and sectarian deity. As with the situation of minority people today, every aspect of life was subject to public scrutiny. This meant that Christian testimony consisted not only of a message spoken aloud to others about Jesus Christ, but also was measured by the quality of the life led by those known to be followers of Jesus.

For Paul, the sphere of Christ's influence extended over the entirety of life. In effect, either one is under the sway of Christ or one is not. "The way of the flesh" (*katà sárka*) is Paul's characteristic designation for a life lived in opposition to Christ. "The way of the Spirit" (*katà pneûma*), however, describes a life consistent with the gospel. The tension between these two ways remains an ongoing challenge even for Christians. The power of sin continues to afflict those who belong to Christ. Yet the Spirit of God is ever present to recreate and direct the lives of the baptized.

The letter to the Romans provides a sterling example of how Paul's theology drives toward a transformed lifestyle. Chapters 1–3 argue for the universality of sin; Jew and Gentile alike are condemned. Justification takes place by faith alone by the power of Christ's death on the cross (Rom 4–5). In baptism we are incorporated into Christ's death and resurrection, which become for us the source of new life (Rom 6). This does not mean we ever become free of sin (Rom 7) but, by the power of God's Spirit at work in us, we are in the process of being transformed (Rom 8).

After an exploration of the problem of Israel's provisional disbelief in Christ (Rom 9–11), Paul concludes the letter with extensive instructions for the Christian life. Similar concerns are discussed at length in virtually every one of his epistles. Chapter 12 begins: "I appeal to you therefore, brothers and sisters, by the mercies of God, to present your bodies as a living sacrifice, holy and acceptable to God, which is your spiritual worship. Do not be conformed to this world, but be transformed by the renewing of your minds, so that you may discern what is the will of God—what is good and acceptable and perfect." The remainder of the letter (Rom 12–16) deals with matters of the Christian lifestyle.

Paul proceeded in both general and specific terms to address the requisites of a life lived in Christ. Consistently, Paul dealt with issues of reconciliation within the community, response to civil authority, the appropriate response to pagan religious practices, sexual ethics, and the law of love for one's neighbor. Though our context is separated significantly in time and space, the dilemmas we face are strikingly analogous as we seek to follow the way of Christ in our lives today. Paul exhorted the recipients of his letters to conform their lives to the image of Christ. Sometimes he gave very specific details about what this should mean in a particular situation. More frequently, however, Paul pointed out a direction to be followed in the spirit of Christ.

While the exact quandaries facing those early Christians are not our own, nevertheless, we are summoned to examine our own lives and measure them according to the way of Jesus Christ. Without becoming bound in legalism, we too are to let the spirit of Christ rule in our hearts. The "epistle of our lives" continues to witness to others about what we say we believe. Love for the neighbor remains the standard Christ left us by which to measure our lives. In our own individual piety, in the Christian *koinonia*, and in the public square, we are made free by the gospel of justification by grace to live out our faith in the way of Christ. When we set out in false directions, the opinion of the whole counsel of God and the wisdom of the Christian community provide checks on our behavior.

Beginning with worship centered on Word and Sacrament, the Christian community moves into the world in mission. Evangelism, global connections, ecumenism, and social ministry each derive from the same impulse that moved Paul to *parenesis*. The Holy Spirit of God wills not only transformed individual lives but a transformed world.

FOR FURTHER READING

Borg, Marcus J. *Jesus: A New Vision: Spirit, Culture, and the Life of Discipleship.* San Francisco: Harper & Row, 1987.

Brueggemann, Walter. *The Prophetic Imagination.* Philadelphia: Fortress, 1978.

Fiorenza, Elizabeth Schüssler. *In Memory of Her: A Feminist Theological Reconstruction of Christian Origin.* New York: Crossroad, 1983.

Furnish, Victor Paul. *Theology and Ethics in Paul.* Nashville and New York: Abingdon, 1968.

Horsley, Richard A. *Jesus and the Spiral of Violence: Popular Jewish Resistance in Roman Palestine.* San Francisco: Harper & Row, 1987.

Meuser, Fred W. *Luther the Preacher.* Minneapolis: Augsburg, 1983.

Perrin, Norman. *Jesus and the Language of the Kingdom: Symbol and Metaphor in New Testament Interpretation.* New York: Harper & Row, 1967.

———. *Rediscovering the Teaching of Jesus.* New York and Evanston: Harper & Row, 1967.

Prenter, Regin. *Spiritus Creator: Luther's Concept of the Holy Spirit.* Philadelphia: Fortress, 1953.

Vajta, Vilmos. *Luther on Worship: An Interpretation.* Philadelphia: Fortress, 1958.

PART TWO

IDENTITY

FOUR

WORSHIP: PRETENDING THE KINGDOM

For some it happens when playing basketball. For others it occurs contemplating great works of art, painting, or music. Among children it happens all the time. When one pretends, the boundaries between the ordinary world and the world of imagination dissolve. In fact, the world of pretend can become so compelling that one totally forgets that any other world even exists. Try calling a child for dinner who is playing house and you may not easily connect. Or observe with what fanaticism supposedly mature people can play a game of cards. For a person with schizophrenia, the fantasy world may not even allow a return to "reality."

These examples are offered to prepare the reader for the interpretation of worship that follows. To pretend is not to do something trivial. To pretend, in the sense here affirmed, is to enter into an alternative world that can profoundly shape and alter the ordinary world. Albert Einstein has been frequently quoted as saying: "Imagination is more important than knowledge." What he meant is that the imagination has the power to so grip our awareness that our lives become forever changed. While it is possible and important to know many things, knowledge is not what changes us. Instead, what changes us are the dreams that grip us, the idea that things do not have to be like they always have been, the power to imagine another course.

When we worship, we enter into such an alternative world. Perhaps we take Sunday mornings so for granted, we no longer realize what is going on. This chapter seeks to reawaken our wonder for the mystery of what God is doing to us as we worship. While we ourselves engage in "pretending" the kingdom of God, God is in the very act of bringing that kingdom to pass!

"IN THE NAME OF ... "

Worship commences in the name of the Father, Son, and Holy Spirit. The invocation of the divine name signals our entry into another time and space, what anthropologists call ritual time and ritual space. Of the many qualities that make for excellence in worship, none is needed more urgently than a profound sense of imagination. As one begins to worship, one must be willing to let down one's defenses, suspend preoccupation with the "real" world, and, like a child, pretend. What we pretend at worship is nothing other than the kingdom of God. At the very same time that we engage in pretending the kingdom, our God is at work by the power of the Spirit to create that very kingdom in our lives and relationships.

Life is punctuated by rituals of many sorts, some so familiar we fail to recognize them as such. Families develop rituals of table blessing and bedtime prayers that interrupt business as usual. Our culture observes rituals rich in symbolism: Valentine's Day with its focus on love, or Halloween with its invocation of supernatural powers that haunt. The nation celebrates its mythology through the rituals of Independence Day and Thanksgiving. What each of these ritual occasions provides is the opportunity to give expression to our deepest convictions, to articulate and rehearse what we ordinarily neglect. When we participate in ritual, the beliefs that daily remain implicit are made explicit. And the course of our lives is altered by the recognition that occurs.

Imagination rests at the heart of ritual. Those who are exceedingly self-conscious have a difficult time letting go of themselves and letting ritual take over. Especially in a culture where self-control is so highly valued, some may feel threatened by ritual performance. Yet in other realms analogies exist that parallel what takes place in worship. Great works of art invite us to enter into an alternative way of viewing the world, which forever alters how we ourselves see things. Games, in which we participate either as players or even as spectators, can become so gripping that we forget who and where we are apart from the playing. Drama, movies, or television programs can lead us to suspend our ordinary worries and so identify with the characters that we laugh and cry along with them.

By the power of the imagination one is able to bring alive things and people that are absent, separated by time or space. Thus, one can become transported out of ordinary circumstances into another realm. People in our culture are hungry to imagine an alternative to this world. Evidence of this deep and desperate hunger abounds. Movies, television programs, spectator sports, computerized virtual reality, and various New Age religious practices each offer the starving imagination nourishment. Through these and other media, the participant exits the realm of the ordinary and enters an alternative world. While visiting there, the individual experiences life through the eyes of an other. There is release from the tensions of the everyday. One's own life and problems are relativized. One begins to view one's own predicament in a new light. New possibilities for thought and action are afforded.

Victor Turner, in his fascinating book *The Ritual Process,* demonstrates interculturally the essential importance of ritual for life. Day by day we live in firmly established orders that provide what Turner calls "structure." Within the structure of life, however, develop hierarchies of power leading to inequity and oppression. Through ritual the ordinary world is, at least temporarily, undone. Ritual time and space offer what Turner calls "communitas," that is, entry into an alternative world, where the structure of ordinary life undergoes reversal. In ritual time and space, the powerful become subject to the powerless, one imagines a peaceable and egalitarian alternative, vexing problems find improbable solutions, and individuals transfer through rites of passage from one life stage into another.

Turner argues that the "liminality" of ritual is a necessary corollary to the structure of ordinary life. The power relations of ordinary life exist in dialectical tension with the alternative world of ritual. In the ritual process, the power structure ruling the everyday becomes relativized. Although at the conclusion of a ritual nothing about the ordinary structure may appear to have been altered, in fact everything is differently arranged. Insight is gained into the way things could and ought to be. The weak are lent hope and the powerful are humbled. Problems are solved. Illnesses are healed. Passage from one status in life to another is authorized.

Although people in contemporary culture demonstrate an immense hunger for ritual time and space, the church often fails to recognize the gift it has to offer in feeding the human imagination. The church through its ritual resources—the church year and the historic liturgy—has nourishment that can truly satisfy the hungry heart. The church has something genuinely worthy of the human imagination—the very kingdom of God. Yet instead of creatively embracing its ritual heritage, it often succumbs to the temptation of overly rationalizing the worship service or takes refuge in "contemporary" services far less ritually satisfying.

What we ritualize by means of the historic Christian liturgy is nothing other than the kingdom of God proclaimed by and embodied in the person of Jesus. As we gather on Sunday morning in the name of the triune God, we enter into ritual time and space and together pretend. We dare to appropriate the very vision of existence that Jesus provided, the vision of the kingdom of God, in which all our conventional wisdom yields to the wisdom of God's mercy and grace. What we pretend is a world in which the gospel of God is truly the very center of our existence.

Simultaneously, the Spirit of God is active with a parallel agenda. Even as we human actors suspend ordinary time in favor of imagining the values of the kingdom, God does even more. God is indeed calling the kingdom of God into being, transforming the stuff of our lives by means of Word and Sacrament. The mystery of worship occurs in the interplay between these two factors: (1) our pretending the kingdom and (2) God's actual creation of the same. This dialectic reflects a new sort of *simul justus et peccator*. We are at the same time pretenders and inheritors of the kingdom of God.

EUCHARISTIC DRAMA

To say that liturgy is the "work of the people" signifies something more profound than congregation members joining to follow an order of worship. As important as it is to have the laity involved in worship—singing, praying, reading, serving—good liturgy entails another dimension, often neglected. The missing element is that of the imagination. When a worshiper gathers in the name of God, he or she covenants to suspend ordinary roles for a time in order to claim his or her ultimate identity. Worship affords the occasion to rehearse the role of one's true self, a citizen of God's kingdom.

Examine the ways in which we pretend the kingdom as we act out the eucharistic drama. By the very invocation of God's presence, we enter into "the kingdom reality." We confess the truth about ourselves, that we are sinners "in thought, word, and deed," who have sinned "by what we have done and by what we have left undone." We do not assume false pretense but admit who we really are, sinful citizens of the kingdom. And we receive God's kingdom pardon with trust and gratitude for Jesus' sake.

We sing hearty kingdom songs of praise to God for all the gifts received. We live out the intention that we are made to glorify God. In the kingdom we implore God for mercy—for ourselves, the church, and the whole world. And we live in the confidence that mercy and peace are exactly what God does provide. We pay attention to God's kingdom word as the central teaching of our lives. The Scripture, originating among the people of God in ancient times and places, becomes again a living word for this gathered people of God today.

In the sermon the preacher invites hearers to imagine the world of the text in such a way that the gospel makes a difference and life is transformed into kingdom. Walter Brueggemann has done much to reawaken us to the imaginative world of the Bible by which our conventional standards yield to kingdom values. The sermon summons us to surrender old grudges that make us bitter, reconcile ourselves to outlandish company, and envision a world in equity and peace. Transformation takes place in the imagining and pretending inspired by the ancient words of Scripture as interpreted by a visionary preacher.

We pledge kingdom allegiance in the words of the Apostles' or Nicene Creed. This confession is not merely on the lips but of the heart, a confession for which loyal citizens would be willing to die. We offer kingdom prayer for the whole people of God in Christ Jesus, and for all people according to their needs. We withhold neither our own deepest needs nor those of our neighbor but let them be known to our gracious God.

We extend a greeting of kingdom peace to one another, especially to those from whom we have been estranged. The kingdom of God is a kingdom of peace in which all are reconciled and joined together in egalitarian community. We offer the first fruits of ourselves, our time, and our possessions in gratitude for the life and blessings God has granted us. This offering is made available for the common good of the kingdom.

New members are received by kingdom washing in the name of Christ. Young and old are incorporated into the body of Christ, under the pledge to dedicate themselves to learning Christ's way and walking in Christ's paths. This faith is affirmed and confirmed as we return time and again to the kingdom promises of grace and forgiveness first uttered by God in baptism. In response to what God has given, citizens of the kingdom commit themselves "to proclaim the good news of God in Christ through word and deed, to serve all people, following the example of our Lord Jesus, and to strive for justice and peace in all the earth."

Kingdom bread is shared around a common table. All are welcome to partake and there is enough for all, to satisfy not only the stomach's hunger but also the heart's. Jesus is present to feed with forgiveness, love, and eternal life. The entire communion of saints, believers of every past age and those from distant places, are present in the eucharistic event. Those who gather in one place are part of a universal company. All join together to pray the kingdom prayer that Jesus taught them.

Friends part with a kingdom blessing from God. Deep in the heart, kingdom peace abides. Citizens of the kingdom move forward in lives of service to God and neighbor.

In the drama of the Eucharist, we pretend that we are already people of the kingdom. In standing and kneeling, singing and listening, washing and eating, praying and blessing, we immerse ourselves in the kingdom of God as envisioned by Jesus. At worship we become parables of kingdom, imagining our lives in community as Jesus would have them.

There are numerous ways in which congregational worship can be enhanced to encourage imaginative pretending of the kingdom. The very use of chant in the liturgy indicates this is a time and place set apart from all others. Nowhere else do we interact with one another in this style. The mood of worship is one of *epiclesis,* invoking and imploring the Spirit of God to come and enliven us by its presence. This means interruptions to worship—announcements, applause, and all else that disturbs the atmosphere of the kingdom—should be kept to a minimum. Silence, by contrast, serves not as an interruption but as the occasion for a potential irruption of the Spirit.

Art and architecture contribute powerfully to the ritual enactment of God's kingdom. The font deserves prominence as the means by which one is washed into the kingdom. The altar is a table, adorned with festive and symbolic paraments for the kingdom meal. Stained glass and vestments speak of the alternative world one enters in worship. The architecture itself should facilitate the congregational drama in which the kingdom is pretended.

Those who plan the worship service do well to select a single theme to highlight on a given Sunday. For example, today we recall that Jesus is the Good Shepherd or today we give thanks for God's gifts in baptism. Accenting a major theme, usually taken from the church year or lectionary, lends focus to the imagination and unites all those who gather for worship. This theme can be announced at the outset and reinforced through the propers for the day. This means careful planning for reinforcing the day's theme in the sermon, prayers, and hymns. Especially meaningful can be the use of the psalm antiphon and an invitation to communion that reinforce the central theme. As the worshipers depart, there is no question about what the congregation has pretended on a given Sunday.

The wonder of worship, however, is greater than what we pretend. We hold the faith that worship is not so much what we do but what God does in Word and Sacrament. If the best we can do is pretend, God can do something better. God takes the materials of our lives and joins them by the power of the Word to create the very kingdom for which we long. Through the word of the gospel and the administration of the sacraments, God activates the forgiveness, deliverance from evil, community, and eternal life that by our power we can only imagine. God produces that which we can only pretend, the real presence of Jesus Christ and his kingdom.

The mystery of worship is that God employs our eucharistic drama as means for spiritual transformation. Regular and frequent worship becomes an imperative for those who would live as citizens of the kingdom. To pray "Thy kingdom come" entails commitment to dedicated rehearsal of one's role. "Practice makes perfect," as they say. As we gather for worship to pretend the kingdom, we gradually find ourselves transformed. Individually, Christ is really present to meet our spiritual needs for forgiveness, hope, and wholeness. Corporately, we discover ourselves being shaped into the body of Christ. God is as alive among us now as in ancient times and places!

"GO IN PEACE, SERVING THE LORD"

The most important thing a congregation does is gather for worship. Participation in worship is the single most important factor in forming Christian *identity*. Moreover, worship contains the energy that transforms congregations into *centers for mission*. As one moves from worship in the sanctuary into the routines of daily life, it is as though one were crossing the border into another land. Our baptism serves as our passport, proving our identity as citizens of the kingdom. Participation in the eucharistic drama issues us a visa that enables our travel in a foreign country.

The concluding exhortation of worship, to "go in peace and serve the Lord," reminds us of the *parenesis* so integral to the Pauline epistles. There lives a dynamic interplay between what takes place at worship and the "liturgy" of daily life. The Christian faith is not something exclusively reserved for Sunday mornings. Nor can it be contained in proper forms, either liturgical or doctrinal. Rather, Christian faith is to be lived out in the daily ministry of all the baptized.

At worship we rehearse life in the kingdom of God. Here one discovers the true self. Among the selves that compete for priority in the human psyche, there exists a self made in the image of Christ. Forgiven, compassionate, and hope-filled, this true self is given expression and nurtured in the experience of Christian liturgy. Nowhere do we feel more at home, more the person God intends us to be, than at worship. Our inmost identity is that of a baptized child of God. We express our true self in confession, absolution, glorifying God, attending to God's Word, offering first fruits to God's service, and partaking of Christ at the holy table.

Similarly, it is at worship that we discover the true nature of human community. Humanity is made by God to live together as a family. All are brothers and sisters with God as nurturing, mentoring parent. In the pretending of the liturgy, we relate to God and one another honestly, freely, and in mutual acceptance. We experience the truth that all are welcome. We find our own gifts affirmed as necessary for the well-being of the body of Christ.

These discoveries about ourselves, God, and the nature of community transform our lives. By our participation in the alternative world of worship, our values and priorities change. Eventually we may discover that we are no longer sure what it means to speak of the "real world." Is the world of ordinary work, family, and routine the "real world"? Or is perhaps the world of worship, the enactment of the kingdom, in a more profound sense the "real world"? Which of these worlds has deeper significance for the ordering of my life? Which of these worlds partakes of eternity and will last forever? We may discover that one day we find ourselves believing that the kingdom's world as imagined in worship is the most real of all.

The life of every congregation occurs in the dynamic relationship between identity formation and the thrust toward mission. Both elements are integral to wholesome congregational life. Both are rooted deeply in the liturgy. Evangelism, global connections, ecumenism, and social ministry each finds its grounding in the kingdom imagined and brought into being in the world of worship.

The impetus to change the world, which is provoked by worship, arises from the dissonance between the values of the conventional world and those of the kingdom of God. The early church acquired a reputation as those who were "turning the world upside down" (Acts 17:6). Conventional values concerning family, wealth, honor, and religion, each are subverted by the wisdom of Jesus—the kingdom and the cross. In this process two dangers can arise: (1) the dissonance is so great as to undermine any serious hope for changing the world and (2) the church domesticates the volatile wisdom of Jesus. Nevertheless, an impulse to world transformation permeates the liturgy.

On an individual scale, I desire to become reconciled with those from whom I am estranged. If God has forgiven me so much and demonstrated infinite mercy by the death of Christ on the cross, then how can I withhold forgiveness from those who have offended me? To deny pardon to one's debtors is to negate the full mercy of Christ and opt instead for the ultimate reality of my resentment. Where conventional wisdom counsels an eye for an eye, the unconventional wisdom of Jesus moves Christian people to forgive as they have been forgiven.

Where every individual longs for guidance in life, the Word of God, read and interpreted at worship, lends orientation and direction. When contemporary lives are juxtaposed with the lives of biblical characters, discoveries are made about the reality of God's grace, enabling new responses to life's challenges. Destructive patterns are unmasked as we witness the foibles of ancient sinners whose motives and behavior are as compromised as our own. Yet the overriding message is of God's mercy, love, and grace, sufficient to amend and redirect even the likes of them—and us. Individuals receive hope and new perspective from the living Word.

As the gospel is proclaimed, sung, prayed, sprinkled, and eaten, an awareness dawns: there is no message like this on earth. The impulse to evangelism also is deeply rooted in worship. Like other types of good news, this best news demands to be shared. There are countless lives that could be enhanced and saved if only this gospel were known and received. Worshipers who experience the gospel of the kingdom and cross are transformed into agents of the *kerygma*. Worship makes evangelists of us, eager to share what we have found.

The prayers of the church foster compassion for the sick, the grieving, the battered, the homeless, and all God's afflicted creatures near at hand. Through the rituals of peace, one is impelled to live as a representative of peace wherever conflict threatens the common good. The offering and shared eucharistic bread instill a sense that everything we have is a gift from God to be shared generously with those in need.

On a corporate scale, worship motivates social ministry. Not everyone will agree about what this means in practice. Many will recognize that the eucharistic drama includes the relief of human suffering from the effects of disasters, famine, and war. Such deeds of charity are a direct consequence of imagining the world as the kingdom of God at worship.

Some will further organize to undertake the excruciating task of transforming the structures of society according to the image of the kingdom. This requires engagement in political movements for change and stirs up controversy about the appropriate relationship between church and state. While it is possible to differ regarding strategies and plans of action, the fundamental impulse to change the world is an authentic consequence of participation in Christian liturgy. The level of frustration experienced by those who carry kingdom values into efforts for social change necessitates both frequent return to liturgical celebration and a healthy sense of humor, as one recognizes the incongruity between the way things are and the way God intends them to be.

Finally, the liturgy moves us to recover the unity of the church. As we confess our faith in one, holy, catholic, and apostolic church, we are reminded of the current dismemberment of Christ's body into competing and often antagonistic factions. As in worship we pretend a "united kingdom," we envision reconciliation of all Christians through dialogue, cooperation, and shared worship. Furthermore, we are reminded that Christian fellowship extends beyond national borders and unites peoples of every race, language, and tribe.

By our participation in worship we receive not only our identity but our mission. The remainder of this book will develop the themes established in this chapter. The theology of the congregation here envisioned—identity and mission—revolves around the experience of the people of God at worship.

FOR FURTHER READING

Collins, Patrick. *Bodying Forth: Aesthetic Liturgy.* New York: Paulist, 1992.

Driver, Tom F. *The Magic of Ritual: Our Need for Liberating Rites that Transform Our Lives and Our Communities.* San Francisco: Harper, 1991.

Kavanagh, Aidan. *On Liturgical Theology.* Collegeville: Pueblo, 1984.

Lathrop, Gordon W. *Holy Things: A Liturgical Theology.* Minneapolis: Fortress, 1993.

Pfatteicher, Philip H. *The School of the Church: Worship and Christian Formation.* Valley Forge, Pa.: Trinity, 1995.

Saliers, Don E. *Worship as Theology: Foretaste of Glory Divine.* Nashville: Abingdon, 1994.

Schmemann, Alexander. *Introduction to Liturgical Theology.* Translated from the Russian by Asheleigh E. Moorhouse. Portland: American Orthodox, 1966.

Senn, Frank C. *Christian Liturgy: Catholic and Evangelical.* Minneapolis: Fortress, 1997.

Turner, Victor. *The Ritual Process: Structure and Anti-Structure.* Chicago: Aldine, 1968.

Wainwright, Geoffrey. *Doxology: The Praise of God in Worship, Doctrine, and Life.* New York: Oxford University Press, 1980.

Zizioulas, John D. *Being as Communion: Studies in Personhood and the Church.* Crestwood, N.Y.: St. Vladimir's Seminary Press, 1985.

FIVE

EDUCATION: MAKING DISCIPLES

Prior to the baptism of children, parents and sponsors promise to bring the baptized faithfully to worship; to teach them the Lord's Prayer, Creed, and Ten Commandments; to place in their hands the Holy Scriptures; and to provide for their instruction in the Christian faith. The object of these promises is to ensure that the baptized live in the covenant of their baptism and in communion with the church and lead godly lives until the day of Jesus Christ. Such promises are easily spoken by those presenting a candidate for baptism. Yet the fulfillment of these promises too often falls by the wayside.

This chapter argues that the number one educational priority of the Christian church is the fulfillment of the baptismal charge: to make disciples of all nations. The risen Jesus left this great commission for the church: "Go therefore and make disciples of all nations, baptizing them in the name of the Father and of the Son and of the Holy Spirit, and teaching them to obey everything that I have commanded you" (Mt 28: 19–20a). While the church over the centuries has been relatively successful with the baptizing portion of this commission, the making of disciples and teaching dimensions have been too often left to happenstance. Responsibility for initiation into Christian belief and practice falls not exclusively to parents but to the entire Christian congregation.

As we undertake the task of Christian education in this generation, there are significant lessons to be learned from the catechetical instruction as practiced in the early centuries of the church. We need to recover the mystery of incorporation into the body of Christ as once practiced through an arcane discipline. Like those early Christian generations, we need the model of saints and martyrs who witness to us the costly nature of Christian discipleship. And we need to focus on how Christian people connect their faith with ministry in daily life. In other words, we need once again to take seriously the Reformation slogan that the church is "the priesthood of all believers."

ARCANE DISCIPLINE

For more than 1,500 years one could presume that Western civilization was based on Christian foundations. The era of Christendom was initiated during the fourth century when Constantine and subsequent Roman emperors gave favored status to the Christian faith. The close alliance of church and state found its apex in the medieval church. Christianity was inseparable from citizenry. The church functioned as a broker of power alongside and frequently in competition with the state. Though much changed with the modern world and the emergence of the nation state as the final arbiter of political power, Christianity continued to provide the religious fiber holding Western society together.

In recent history, however, there is a cacophony of voices declaring that the age of Christendom has come to an end. Not only is our age described as postmodern but also post-Christian. This means that one can no longer assume that Christianity serves as the least common denominator binding together Western culture. This analysis of the present moment of history is held not only by agnostic intellectuals but by one of the foremost interpreters of the contemporary Christian church, Loren Mead.

In *The Once and Future Church,* Mead sets forth his understanding of the dilemma facing the contemporary church. In short, we are presently experiencing the collapse of the "Christendom paradigm" of the church. Under this paradigm the church lived in close identification with the surrounding culture; being Christian was equated with being a good citizen to a large degree. The congregation saw itself as a parish, "taking care" of the membership that lived in its precinct. Mission was something that happened in distant places among foreign people.

Mead contends that many of the struggles now facing the church result from the dissolution of these presuppositions of Christendom. Even if it once were true, no longer can one dare to assume that everyone is a Christian. Nor can one assume that civic society is a direct expression of Christian values. This, in turn, means that mission is not merely a task undertaken in distant places by trained missionaries, but rather something that is an imperative close to home.

The crisis of the church is that we are already experiencing the consequences of this new post-Christendom situation yet do not know how to proceed in a way that meets the immediate challenge. In his book, Mead also sketches the outline of an earlier model, that of the pre-Constantine church, which he calls the "apostolic paradigm."

Members of the church, according to this paradigm, belonged on the basis of personal conviction and commitment, not by virtue of birth in a particular territory. The boundary existing between church and culture was well-defined. One took a deliberate and risky stance in entering the Christian fellowship. Often the prevailing culture lived in antagonism to the church, expressing its hostility through acts of persecution.

The contention of this chapter is that in our current situation we have much to learn from the early church, Mead's "apostolic paradigm," in terms of Christian education. Though the form of Christendom remains intact, its substance is in the process of disintegrating. Evidence of this dilemma is available from several quarters. One of the studies most pertinent to this theme was undertaken by the Search Institute under the title "Effective Christian Education: A National Study of Protestant Congregations." The conclusions of this study reinforce the idea that the inner substance of the Christian faith within the church is dissolving.

The Search Institute study measures maturity of faith according to two criteria: a horizontal component of devotion to serving the neighbor and a vertical component characterized by a deep and personal relationship to God. Among adults in the Protestant denominations studied, most registered a lack of mature faith according to this standard. An even larger number of adolescents demonstrated what the study calls "undeveloped faith." While there appears to be a direct correlation between aging and an increasingly developed faith outlook, another factor emerged as especially significant for contributing to faith maturity, that is, participation in Christian education. The single most important thing a congregation can do to promote faith development is to provide effective Christian education programming.

Christian education must be seen and understood as a lifelong undertaking. This must not only be held as an ideal but be put into practice, with adults setting the model for the youth. The quantity of educational programs is not as important as the quality of the programs that are offered. A congregation is better served to develop excellence in leadership and content in its educational programs rather than providing numerous offerings shallow in quality. A key issue disclosed in the Search study is the faith maturity of the teacher. Participants advance most significantly in their own faith development under the direction of a teacher who demonstrates highly developed faith.

At no time in the church's history did it devote more deliberate attention to Christian education than in its first three centuries. Catechesis took place in a lengthy process leading to baptism during the Easter vigil. Catechumens only gradually were initiated into the mysteries of the Christian faith. For example, those preparing for baptism might be allowed to come to worship to hear the Scripture and sermon, but they were dismissed prior to the celebration of the Eucharist. Exposure to the mystery of the Eucharist was something for which one had to be carefully seasoned. The intensive catechetical process might last as long as three years with converts carefully nurtured into ever deeper understanding of Christian truth and practice.

In the twentieth century, Dietrich Bonhoeffer sparked renewed interest in the relevance of a *disciplina arcana* (literally, "secret discipline") with some fascinating references in his *Letters and Papers from Prison.* Isolated from traditional forms of Christian community, Bonhoeffer speculated about a "religionless" Christianity in a "world come of age." Already it seems Bonhoeffer discerned the end of Christendom in his experience of Nazi Germany. While publicly a church, practicing arcane discipline, would not (or could not) perform cultic or ritual acts (being fully integrated into worldly service), privately there would remain a "secret discipline" by which the church would constitute its Christian identity. By means of an arcane discipline initiating them into the way of discipleship, Christians attain maturity of faith and become prepared to live out their faith in the public, non-Christian world.

The contemporary church needs a recovery of the sense of otherness of the Christian faith as evoked through the practice of an arcane discipline. The Christian faith is not a subject easily mastered, certainly not by adolescent confirmands or even their middle-aged parents. To believe and to live as a Christian is something distinct from the assumptions and lifestyles of the surrounding culture. The journey into Christian discipleship is a lifelong endeavor. There are ever new mysteries and nuances of the faith to explore. In our approach to Christian education, we must exude a sense of the wonder at the depths of Christian wisdom, that presents a challenge to all ages of discovering new dimensions and applications of the Christian mystery.

Three words summarize the goals of an effective congregational Christian education program: to *learn,* to *think,* and to *live* the Christian story. In everything a congregation does, there should prevail the awareness that being Christian is something unique and distinct. For those familiar with the work of James W. Fowler, these three goals—learning, thinking, and living the story—can be correlated with the six stages of faith that he articulates. Fowler argues that one's understanding of faith develops in formal stages that are related to human cognitive and psychosocial development. One proceeds in faith development through consecutive stages, not being able to bypass any given stage, but certainly able to become fixed at a certain stage which never is surpassed. While Fowler identifies six formal stages, we here focus on three educational goals.

The first task of Christian education is to assist children and members to *learn* the Christian story. This means a strong emphasis on learning Bible stories in pre-school and elementary years with only secondary attention given to explanation of what stories mean. Music and art are marvelous media for effectively reinforcing basic Bible content. Not just a few stories but the entire biblical narrative should be told, even those stories from which initially we think children ought to be sheltered. It is during the elementary years that basic knowledge of the catechism should also be mastered; perhaps each school year focusing on a specific chapter, for example, Ten Commandments in first grade, Lord's Prayer in second, and so on.

Among adults this educational goal can be accomplished through programs that focus on the mastery of Bible content. There are several excellent programs of this genre, or a knowledgeable teacher can simply accompany a group in reading through the entire Bible. The primary educational goal at this level is to learn the biblical and catechetical story of God's immense mercy for the world as demonstrated in the narrative.

A second educational goal is to *think* through the story. If confirmands already have a firm grasp of the biblical story, critical reflection ought to be a major emphasis of confirmation instruction. To think through the story entails introduction to the historical process through which the Scriptures developed, that is, basic introduction to historical interpretation. It means discovering the nature of myth as a conveyor of God's truth as one thinks about certain Bible stories, for example, Jonah and the whale. It means confronting the apparent discrepancy between what one learned about creation from the first chapters of Genesis and what one is learning about the big bang and the theory of evolution from scientists.

The church must demonstrate a willingness to accompany its members, especially the young, as they critically examine the truth of the Christian faith, while at the same time testifying that such critical thought does not so much diminish as enhance the meaning of Christian truth. The church is failing in its educational mission insofar as it hesitates and avoids grappling with these issues. By failing to prepare its youth for reflection on such critical questions, the church unwittingly assures that each generation undergoes a period of disillusionment before some—but only some—find their way back into its fold.

Adult educational forums are the ideal place to assist all members to critically think through the basis of their faith. Since not all will participate in such ventures, sermons can regularly assist in demonstrating the church's willingness to delve into critical examination of its beliefs. Likewise in its publications (for example, a monthly newsletter), a congregation can provide guidance for deepening awareness of the complexity of Christian history and thinking through difficult questions. Classes for new members should place significant emphasis on the importance of lifelong Christian education and provide the occasion for serious intellectual inquiry.

In accomplishing the goal of encouraging people to think through the faith, opportunity should be offered for exposing members to great Christian thinkers from the past and present, those who both analyzed the faith with critical acumen and maintained sincere devotion. Justin Martyr, Augustine, Hildegaard of Bingen, Thomas Aquinas, Theresa of Avila, Martin Luther, Søren Kierkegaard, Dorothy Day, Dietrich Bonhoeffer, and Gustavo Gutiérrez are among those whose reflections on the faith deserve to be widely known. More about the importance of the witness of Christian saints will be developed in the next section.

Finally, the church must engage its members in the endless task of *living* the faith. As we have seen, participation in the liturgy provides major impetus for this goal. Never do we leave behind our sinful and selfish nature, which limits our ability to exemplify a Christlike life. Yet those who are mature in faith demonstrate a powerful congruity between what they profess and how they live. Each sanctified life finds its own expressions, given the unique gifts of God and the particular station in God's world. The Spirit of God becomes manifest powerfully in lives humbly submitted to divine service. The central sign of a saintly life is always the admission of one's sinfulness before God and neighbor, accompanied by joyous reception of God's grace and forgiveness granted in Christ Jesus. "I have been crucified with Christ; and it is no longer I who live, but it is Christ who lives in me" (Gal 2: 19b–20).

Our education in the Christian faith leads us back again and again to the Sunday morning liturgy. This remains for a lifetime the central location where one is educated in what it means to be a child of God and a member of the Christian community. In the regular rhythm of Word and Sacrament, we learn, think, and live the faith.

SAINTS WHO FOLLOWED

Our age is hungry for heroes. Every news story seems to shift away from an analysis of issues and reasons to the personalities of those involved. Movie stars, athletes, musicians, politicians, military officers, and announcers each have a place in the pantheon of American gods. The values that these heroes represent are glamour, wealth, strength, power, sex appeal, and success. Young people are not the only ones drawn to these as their role models, although the tendency of us all is especially noticeable among them. Heroes from the screen serve as mighty icons in shaping our aspirations and, thereby, our self-image and identity.

Over the generations, Christians have engaged in heated controversy over the place afforded to its "heroes," the saints. Here the term "saint" is not used so much in the generic sense in which all the baptized are saints but in the particular sense that some become exemplary for others in demonstrating the meaning of the Christian life. Some argue, with good reason, that the only figure deserving our undivided attention is the person of Jesus alone. Jesus Christ is the exclusive object of our devotion. And in terms of our worship, clearly this position is correct.

Yet while it is proper and true that Jesus be and remain the central Christian icon, is there not also room for amazement and inspiration from the example of those who in every generation demonstrated what it means to live a Christian life? There is a deep and profound longing for such models. If they are not forthcoming from the church, then heroes will be sought elsewhere and emulated according to values that contradict the faith.

The testimony of the saints offers a tremendous resource for Christian education. Whereas abstract discussion of religious doctrine and theological concepts is perceived as dull and irrelevant, to enliven the discussion through biographical study, to demonstrate that the teachings of the church meant something to real people in a real moment in history, makes a tremendous impression. James W. McClendon is certainly right. Theology as incarnated in a personal biography reveals how ideas do indeed make a difference in how one lives. The dilemmas faced by other Christians as they sought to remain faithful disciples in their own context, sheds light on our struggle to be faithful here and now.

McClendon demonstrates his case with reference to the biographies of Dag Hammarskjöld, Martin Luther King, Jr., Clarence Jordan, and Charles Ives. He pays strict attention to the central images that guided each journey in faith. For example, Hammarskjöld favored the images of servant, Jesus as Brother, and the "unheard of," while King turned to images of the exodus—Egyptian bondage, the Pharaoh's yoke, and the promised land. Certain guiding images shaped a particular way of envisioning and imagining the faith in order to meet the particular challenges of Christian discipleship that confronted each of them.

This method can bear fruit as the commitment and example of myriad saints feed the imaginations of Christian people. Saints from biblical times testify to God's presence in diverse contexts: Elijah, Ruth, Jeremiah, Esther, Mary Magdalene, and Barnabas. Each points to a story worth repeating. The history of the church is replete with the witness of those committed to following Jesus: Gregory of Nyssa, Macrina, Francis of Assisi, Clare, Margery Kempe, Anselm of Canterbury, John Calvin, Rose of Lima, Ann Lee, Jonathan Edwards, Sojourner Truth, Dietrich Bonhoeffer, and Mother Theresa. To view their lives in the context of their times is to shed light on our own lives and times. As we consider these witnesses, what does it mean for us to be disciples of Jesus today?

These saints demonstrate not only that in every generation there have been those who translated the faith to meet the challenges of their own times, but also that in every age it is the same God and the same Christ to whom the church seeks to remain faithful. Above all, we learn that God has remained faithful to us and that where sin has invaded the lives of the saints, God's forgiveness has been abundant. We learn that now it is our turn to find the proper images for living faithfully in this generation.

Those who employ biography as a means of Christian education will discover a vitality missing from discussions of disembodied ideas. Biography provides an entrance to the discussion of concepts that remain vital for Christian identity and mission. Audio-visual presentations provide further assistance in envisioning the lives of the saints. In this process, Christian people fill their minds with alternative images of heroes, who aid them in discerning how to live their own lives Christianly. At worship we reinforce these images by observing the lives of those saints recognized in the liturgical calendar.

This educational emphasis on the lives of the saints should not overlook the testimony of saints closer to home. There is much wisdom to be discovered where congregations establish various mentoring programs among members. Baptismal sponsors should understand themselves as mentors for the godchild. Confirmands can be assigned mentors to nurture them in faith development. The newly married can be paired with experienced couples who will pray for them and encourage them. The grieving receive consolation and understanding from those who themselves have experienced similar grief.

The work of the saints goes on in every Christian congregation. In groups formed for mutual support, there exists an educational component demonstrating Christian response to life's crises. The relationships that form among members teach volumes about the ongoing incarnation of the faith. It is especially through the example of those who walk with us as mentors and friends that we learn how to live the Christian life. Congregations do well to name, organize, and otherwise foster mentor relationships among members and to recognize these as a valuable component of educational ministry.

CROSSINGS

One of the most impenetrable boundaries of life is the one dividing Sunday morning from the rest of the week. Increasingly in the modern world, the relevance of faith to daily life has become marginalized. The nineteenth century, which saw the industrial revolution flourish, was the same century that witnessed the privatization (and in that context the "feminization") of the church. Faith came to be understood as good for families, especially for women and children in domestic life, but Christian commitment had no place in the workaday world. The remnants of this view persist to the present. Note the relative absence of men from Sunday worship and the startling statistic that correlates continued church involvement among youth with the active participation of their fathers.

At least since the Reformation, the church has elevated this watchword: "the church is the priesthood of all believers." By this, Luther meant to sanctify the vocations of all Christians, placing great importance on the role of all honest work in ordering and sustaining God's world. Today we sometimes speak of "ministry in daily life" as an expression of this Reformation concern. Nevertheless, to an alarming degree the bifurcation between Sunday morning and the rest of the week remains fixed.

Congregations must address this gap in their educational ministry. Models exist in the "Crossings" ministry of St. Louis and the "Connections" program (created by Norma Cook Everist and Nelvin Vos), which have proven invaluable in crossing the boundary between what we profess and the occupations into which we pour out our lifeblood. By means of these models, members of congregations are asked to conscientiously juxtapose their faith and their vocations. Many do so for the first time. In a process of explicit reflection, new insight is gained not only into the relevance of the faith for daily life but into the meaning of faith as one's very source of identity. The Scripture comes alive as testimony to God's involvement, not in ecclesiastical affairs, but in the lives of people engaged in nothing less than their daily business.

Groups can be formed for mutual sharing about the interface of faith and daily work. Bible texts can be studied in terms of their impact on integrating faith into the daily ethical and interpersonal dilemmas facing Christians in the world. Through attempts to bring the workplace into the sanctuary grow relationships of mutual support that occur at a profound level. Other groups evolve that continue to meet for prayer and guidance. People who once believed they were too busy for church now see it as the necessary foundation for functioning with integrity, learning to deal with failure, and discovering transcendent meaning within the daily grind. The liturgy becomes the lens through which all of life becomes transfigured.

Each of the three emphases discussed in this chapter—the mindset of the early church with its arcane discipline translated today into the basic goals of learning, thinking, and living the Christian story; the importance of saints as models of the faith in practice; and the connection between Sunday worship and daily life—contributes not only to better Christian education but to the renewal of the church in a post-Christian age. The number one priority for Christian education in our time is disciple-making. While the number of directions one can follow in Christian education are infinite, this priority contributes directly to the fundamental purpose of the congregation, building Christian identity for the sake of Christ's mission in the world.

FOR FURTHER READING

Benson, Peter L., and Eklin, Carolyn H. *Effective Christian Education: A National Study of Protestant Congregations.* A Summary Report of Faith, Loyalty, and Congregational Life. Minneapolis: Search Institute, 1990.

Everist, Norma Cook. *Education Ministry in the Congregation: Eight Ways We Can Learn from One Another.* Minneapolis: Augsburg, 1983.

Everist, Norma Cook, and Vos, Nelvin. *Connections: Faith and Life.* Chicago: Evangelical Lutheran Church in America, Division for Congregational Ministries, 1997.

Fowler, James W. *Stages of Faith and Religious Development: Implications for Church, Education and Society.* New York: Crossroad, 1991.

Groome, Thomas H. *Christian Religious Education: Sharing Our Story and Vision.* San Francisco: Harper & Row, 1981.

Hardy, Lee. *Fabric of This World: Inquiries into Calling, Career Choice, and the Design of Human Work.* Grand Rapids: Eerdmans, 1990.

McClendon, James William, Jr. *Biography as Theology: How Life Stories Can Remake Today's Theology.* Nashville: Abingdon, 1974.

Mead, Loren B. *Five Challenges for the Once and Future Church.* Bethesda: Alban Institute, 1996.

———. *The Once and Future Church: Reinventing the Congregation for a New Mission Frontier.* Bethesda: Alban Institute, 1991.

Rite of Christian Initiation of Adults: Study Edition. Prepared by International Commission on English in Liturgy and Bishops' Committee on the Liturgy. Washington, D.C.: United States Catholic Conference, 1988.

SIX

FELLOWSHIP: FRIENDS OF THE CRUCIFIED

On Maundy Thursday the liturgy engages the congregation in two profound ritual actions. The first happens only on this night. Girded with a towel, a minister takes water and bends down to wash feet. This ritual reenacts the night before Jesus' crucifixion as he humbled himself to wash the feet of his disciples.

Prior to the foot-washing ritual, a passage of Scripture is read from the Gospel of John, chapter 13: "I have given you a new commandment, that you love one another. Just as I have loved you, you also should love one another. By this everyone will know that you are my disciples, if you have love for one another" (vv. 34-35). Elaborating on this theme in 16:12-15, Jesus declares: "This is my commandment, that you love one another as I have loved you. No one has greater love than this, to lay down one's life for one's friends. You are my friends if you do what I command you. I do not call you servants any longer, because the servant does not know what the master is doing; but I call you friends, because I have made known to you everything that I have heard from my Father."

The second ritual action of Maundy Thursday is the gathering around the table for Holy Communion. Bread and wine are shared, the very body and blood of Christ, in remembrance of all Jesus suffered to demonstrate the depths of God's love for us.

Together these rituals, the washing of feet accompanied by a reading about love and the gathering together around the table, establish the norm for fellowship in a congregation. Friendship with the crucified Jesus serves as the basis for our friendship with one another. When we view one another properly, we see the other in the light of what Jesus suffered for each of us on the cross. We understand one another as common recipients of divine grace as we partake together from the Lord's table. And we comprehend that our only mission is exemplified in the washing of feet, the weary feet of those within the congregation and the feet of many others whom we invite to be refreshed in Christian fellowship.

THE MEANING OF CHRISTIAN FRIENDSHIP

To describe members of a congregation as "friends" can lead to serious misunderstanding. Friendship in Christ is not founded on "feelings" of closeness to one another. Nor is it based on one's attraction to certain kindred personalities. In the surrounding culture, friendship is based almost exclusively upon what one finds appealing in another person. Friendship focuses upon what friends can offer to each other to achieve self-fulfillment. Friendship is reduced to seeking out persons who can help satisfy my personal needs.

Instead, in the church, we must begin to think christologically about friendship. Friendship begins with Jesus graciously naming us as his friends. Those who seek to follow Jesus and keep his commandments are given the privilege of understanding themselves as Jesus' friends. This sounds at first rather cozy. Me and Jesus: friends. That is, until we notice those others whom Jesus also calls friends. To be summoned into friendship with Jesus is to discover ourselves in the company of all those who live as Jesus' disciples. Many of these are people with whom we would by natural inclination never associate.

As Dietrich Bonhoeffer wrote in *Life Together,* Christian community is not a dream of our own making. Christian friendship comes into existence not according to my own ideal expectations but rather at God's beckoning. One of the greatest threats to genuine Christian community is the "visionary dreaming" by which I establish my own standards for the community, rather than allowing the spirit of Christ to create the community according to God's own specifications.

One of the deepest mysteries of Christian friendship occurs as Jesus Christ himself meets us in the form of the other. Article 4 of the Smalcald Articles lists five means by which the gospel of Jesus Christ is mediated to us, one of these being "the mutual conversation and consolation of the brethren." Jesus promised in Matthew 18:20, "Where two or three are gathered in my name, I am there among them." As Christians speak to one another in mutual faith, sharing mutual concerns and addressing one another under the gospel's promise of forgiveness, Jesus is really present among them. Thus occurs the miracle that we become "little Christs" for one another (Luther).

M. Scott Peck retells a powerful tale, "The Rabbi's Gift," at the beginning of his book *The Different Drum: Community Making and Peace.* A once thriving monastery has over the decades been reduced to five aged monks. The abbot broods over the decimation of the once vital order, pondering its imminent demise. Going to the woods to pray, the abbot consults with an old rabbi there on retreat. As they commiserate about days gone by, the abbot beseeches the rabbi for advice. The rabbi's only cryptic word is this: "One of you is the Messiah."

Returning to the monastery, the abbot shares this word with the brothers. In consternation, none of them can believe this could be true: they know one another's faults all too well! Yet slowly and surely there develops a profound sense of respect for one another, just in the slight chance the rabbi could be right. This new sense of respect and self-dignity begins to attract new visitors to the dying monastery. One by one, new postulants enter, restoring the order as a center of hope in the lives of many. What wonders are wrought by the conviction that in my neighbor I meet Jesus Christ!

The mystery of friendship in Christ goes yet deeper. As we live together in Christian community, Jesus promises to be present in our relationships. Yet we are not the ones with the power to decide when and where Jesus becomes manifest. Rather, as Jesus indicated in the parable of the great judgment in Matthew 25:31-46, it is at the moment we would least expect it, in the person of the "least of these," in the form of the hungry, sick, or imprisoned one, that Jesus comes to encounter us. This passage summons us to extend Christian friendship to those at the very margins of "decent" society. To establish a congregation as an association of the "like-minded" is likely to exclude Christ as the one who meets us in the form of the unlovely. We are summoned to be a church that is radically egalitarian in its composition, inviting those the world scorns.

Finally, Christian friendship entails communion with the crucified. A theology of the cross insists that Jesus is never more present than in those very places where he appears to be most absent. Crucified as a criminal on Golgotha, Jesus was rejected by all decent society and even abandoned by his disciples. Yet exactly here God was manifest in our world, taking up the cause of all this world's abandoned and rejected ones. Christian friendship takes up the cause of Jesus by ministering to those in acute pain and suffering. Friendship in the church of Jesus Christ searches for those places of service where no one else dares go—among those most excluded from human company. Here it is that one can be assured that Jesus Christ is already present, waiting for a cruciform church to appear.

EGALITARIAN COMMUNION

Members of a congregation do not have to like one another, although that is always nice. They do, however, have the command from Jesus to love one another. As in a family with several children, they don't have to like one another. But God has thrust them together into this configuration, and they are compelled to learn the true nature of love, not as a romantic ideal but a daily challenge. In a family, there is no question about choosing to belong or not belong. Belonging is a given, and one simply learns to get along with each other's quirks and bad manners. The church, like a family, serves as a clinic for discovering what it means to be brothers and sisters.

The primary arena where we learn the art of Christian fellowship is the liturgy. By our common participation in the rituals of confession, absolution, prayer, passing the peace, and sharing Eucharist—as we pretend together the kingdom—we see one another differently, that is, truly, as we really are in God's eyes. The distinctions that divide and separate us according to the standards of the world are radically altered by our common baptism in the name of Jesus. Neither age, nor gender, nor race, nor sexual orientation, nor wealth, nor job status deserves any consequence (Gal 3:28). The only relevant information is that we are all people for whom Christ died.

When the leadership of worship is shared with the active involvement of many assisting ministers as ushers, greeters, acolytes, cantors, choir members, lectors, musicians, intercessors, and communion assistants, another key aspect of Christian fellowship is disclosed. The people of God are a gifted people; spiritual gifts abound in the fellowship. Each has been granted by God special gifts symbolized by the services rendered by various members at worship. The standard by which these gifts are measured is the contribution they make to the common good. The gifts God lends are not for personal aggrandizement but for the mutual upbuilding of the body of Christ. Paul's dictum regarding spiritual gifts continues to instruct us: "the greatest of these is love" (1 Cor 13:13).

While the expression of spiritual gifts is symbolized by mutuality in the leadership of liturgy, the sharing of gifts is extended by the mutual care of members throughout the week. Relationships of friendship are witnessed in the concern shown for those members of the body of Christ in special need: the sick, the dying, the grieving, the divorcing, the unemployed, the hungry, the single parents, the infertile couples, the spiritually confused, the troubled youth, and so forth.

As members of a congregation live together and experience mutual needs, they discover the particular gifts of the various individuals. One is gifted in sewing, another in carpentry, yet another in leading small groups. Each individual has unique charisms to offer. Unlike society, which marginalizes all those who are not "normal," that is, young, successful, and healthy, the fellowship of the church preaches and aims to practice an egalitarian communion, in which the gifts of each are employed for common benefit. The community that gathers around Jesus is a motley crew, unlovely in the world's eyes but saints according to divine promise.

This is not to say conflicts do not arise among members of the Christian fellowship. Tensions do arise both from chafing personalities and from differing opinions about decisions to be made. It is always tragic when congregation members cannot resolve the differences that divide them. Slapping labels on those with whom one is in conflict is never helpful. Instead, mediation that assists in viewing issues from the perspective of the other, while perhaps not always resolving the difference, can teach us to respect one another and preserve the overall aim of promoting the common good. Where antagonism leads to the division of the congregation, all parties need to confess their own sins and beg for God's gracious forgiveness.

Prayer serves to powerfully create and sustain Christian friendship within the congregation. While prayer remains integral to Sunday worship, mutual prayer continues throughout the week. The constant offering of intercessions for one another reflects the divine context in which the congregation lives. The special needs of the sick, grieving, and distressed are brought to God in prayer, and we are shaped in the process. Prayer moves us to acts of charity on behalf of those for whom we pray. We visit, call, or send a meal. Anger is diffused in prayer; those who are praying for one another cannot easily harbor resentment.

Prayer for the congregation leads to transformed action on each other's behalf. Through shared participation in worship and mutual concern rooted in prayer, a congregation becomes, in the parlance of the Quakers, a society of friends. One definition of a friend is someone with whom you enjoy "wasting" time. Where caring relationships develop among members, there is heaven on earth. So too is there extreme disillusionment where the church fails to live up to its potential as a loving community. Many are those who have become alienated from the church due to its failure to care. Indeed, for its lack of genuine fellowship, the church must continually confess its sins and plead for God's mercy. One acute danger of Christian friendship is that it cease to be welcoming of the outsider. Members become so familiar with one another that they fail to extend fellowship beyond a closed circle. The standard of egalitarian communion fails to be normative even in the sanctuary.

Christian fellowship begins and ends with the friendship of God in Christ with us. For Jesus' sake we call one another friends. This means patterning the relationships of the church after the manner of Jesus: egalitarian, compassionate, listening, serving, forgiving, celebrating the gifts of each, cruciform, caring for the least. Friendship always remains both an incomparable joy for which to give thanks and a responsibility for bearing another's burdens. As it is in our own friendship with Jesus, so may it be in the communion of saints.

PASTOR AND PEOPLE

One way of understanding the pastoral office is to view the pastor as public representative of the friendship of God among a people. The pastor is called to publicly proclaim God's gospel friendship in Word and Sacrament. And the pastor is called to embody the friendship of God in relationships with members of a congregation, especially through pastoral care.

The pastor, by virtue of her/his office, holds one of the most privileged positions in all of society. Invited into the lives of people at moments of great vulnerability and joy, a pastor serves as a representative of God in everything that is said and done. While one should resist losing one's individual identity to the requirements of an office, graciously assuming the role that inevitably comes with the office opens great opportunities for ministry. The work of a pastor is a vocation, not a job that can be set aside at the end of a work day. Whether at the local fast food restaurant or shopping at a mall, members and non-members alike will see the person as pastor, God's representative.

This not only places a burden of responsibility on the shoulders of the individual called to ordained ministry but, where a family is involved, can also encumber the entire family system. Spouses and children of pastors suffer from a stigma that must first be acknowledged before it can be creatively addressed. While it is important to maintain one's integrity and not surrender to unrealistic demands, a pastor's family has to adjust to its public identity as graciously as possible. Support from other clergy families, understanding from sensitive congregation members, and a sense of humor are assets in this process.

The privilege afforded the pastor, to enter into the private hurts and celebrations of God's people, entails responsibility as well. As a giver of pastoral care, the pastor must be trained in listening and responding to human need. The pastor, like the suffering servant of Isaiah, is acquainted with sorrows and familiar with grief (53:3). Unlike the friends of Job, the pastor refrains from answering in platitudes, and instead allows the full measure of human emotion to find expression. Sometimes this means the anger people feel toward God will be directed instead at one's own person as God's representative. In these cases, this is a function of the office one bears rather than a matter to be taken personally.

In the pursuit of appropriate pastoral care, the pastor should not presume to be the master of all human dilemmas. Through experience, the pastor will be exposed to a wide range of human problems and predicaments. To properly distinguish between law and gospel has implications for pastoral care. A word of judgment may sometimes be necessary to remove a person from a destructive path. Most often, the pastor will seek ways of making the comfort and forgiveness of God known in the lives of people distressed. One of life's greatest needs is hope for a better future, and the pastor can provide such, for in the friendship of God there is always hope. Should the situation call for skills beyond the competence of the pastor, a mark of wisdom is to know one's limits and be aware of the available resources in order to make a helpful referral.

With the pastor's privileged access to people's lives comes also the requirement not to use one's authority destructively. This can occur in conversations with members who do not share the same level of knowledge as the educated pastor. It can occur in meetings where group dynamics single out certain individuals for ostracism if they oppose the pastor. Most tragically, it can occur in relationships with parishioners who become objects of sexual manipulation. Sexual contact with a congregation member always constitutes a violation of pastoral trust and is destructive of the church's fellowship. The sacred trust necessary for the pastor to serve as representative of God's friendship is betrayed. Abuse of pastoral power is always a cause for church discipline. The healing process within a congregation is lengthy and arduous.

One of the lost customs in modern society is that of making house calls. Visitation by the pastor serves as symbol of the friendship of God meeting people in their home space. While scheduling around the activities of busy members presents a challenge, the value of such visitation is finally worth the hassle. A foundation for ministry is built as a pastor is welcomed as guest and friendship is extended. The focus of pastoral calling is not only to learn the life story of the members of the congregation but to communicate the friendship of God with each individual and family, especially in response to stories of pain. This entails conversation about the spiritual needs of persons as well as about physical health. Taking time for Bible reading, hymn singing, and prayer as part of a pastoral visit communicates the nearness and mercy of God for those in each home.

Pastoral friendship also means faithful and prompt response at moments of acute need. Those hospitalized, anticipating surgery, grieving a loss, or in any type of crisis need the reassurance of God's presence by contact from their pastor and other Christians. Though such occasions always come as interruptions to the planned schedule, they are the very times when God becomes mysteriously present in a remarkable manner. The pastor is privileged to witness to the unfailing power of God to sustain us in life's most challenging hour. Sharing prayer or private communion places the entire crisis in a different perspective, that of God's unceasing kindness and friendship. Pastors who respond faithfully to the acute needs of people make tremendous testimony to the goodness and mercy of the One they represent.

The telephone provides another important avenue for extending the friendship of God among the members of a congregation. A quick phone call in the course of the day does much to buoy another's spirit. People appreciate being remembered, whether it be on a birthday, anniversary, retirement, or some other notable occasion. Those recently hospitalized can give a follow-up report over the phone. Contact with new or lapsed members can be initiated. Creative use of the telephone can serve to broaden pastoral ministry in communicating God's friendship among a people.

The purpose of congregational ministry among youth is not to create a ghetto of younger aged persons but to integrate them into the larger fellowship and ministry of the congregation. Too often youth ministry degenerates into "activities" to keep the "young people" occupied and off the streets. The youth group functions more like a social club than an aspect of the entire congregation's life. The youth of a congregation are not "its future" as many are wont to say, but already baptized and full members of the body of Christ.

In subtle and sometimes overt ways, most congregations communicate a second-class status to their youth programs. They hire an "assistant" pastor to entertain the youth. Or they have to coerce members to take over as youth sponsors. They hold a "Youth Sunday" or have special services for the youth. In and of themselves none of these practices are inherently bad, but they communicate a mindset that steals from the church the plenitude of gifts that youth bring to make the body of Christ healthy and sound. The gifts that unique and individual young people bring to the church are needed by the entire congregation and should not be relegated to a youth enclave.

From a young age children should be welcome in the church's fellowship. Children should grow up knowing their congregation as a place where they belong and are cherished as persons who share the common identity of baptized children of God with all members of whatever age. Children, as part of the congregation, should be welcome at worship, even if this means they sometimes interrupt the proceedings. There is no reason families with children should be expected to occupy the back pews of the sanctuary when the action is taking place up front. Encourage them to sit toward the front. Hymns that children enjoy can be sung by the entire congregation. Children's sermons can be based on the regular lectionary and make points applicable to members of every age, rather than merely offer trite entertainment. Children can serve as acolytes, choir members, greeters, ushers, and readers, having received comparable training and attained the level of competence expected of all members.

Children can be welcomed at Holy Communion, if not by receiving the elements, then by means of a personal blessing. Preparation for the Lord's table can be done at an earlier age than many congregations now practice. As soon as they can read, children can be presented their own Bibles within the context of the worship service. Younger children display an enthusiasm for Bible reading that often puts their elders to shame. Children should be frequently reminded of the importance of their own baptism as they participate in the order of baptism for others, especially babies. As they repeat the liturgy on a regular basis, children soon become active participants in the eucharistic drama. There is deep joy for those who lead worship to look into the congregation and see children singing along with the rest.

By the time one reaches the age of confirmation instruction, children should already be at home in the congregation's life. In addition to learning to think more deeply about the Christian faith during confirmation classes, regular classes deserve to be "distracted" as confirmands bring experiences from daily life to the classroom. These can be considered from the standpoint of how one deals with a particular issue as a Christian. It is the friendship of God experienced in the relationship of confirmands with their teachers and pastor that will encourage ongoing participation even when the formal classes are completed.

Post-confirmation youth need to be fully incorporated into the congregation's ministry. While they may continue to hold separate meetings, it is essential that they also be intentionally included in congregational worship, education, fellowship, and other programs. Young people are often extremely willing and enthusiastic participants in service projects to meet the needs of others. Young people can be encouraged to participate actively in congregational committees and celebrations. A fine symbol of equal status is to elect young members to serve on the governing council.

Youth ministry in the congregation should not be separate from the rest of ministry but a vital dimension within the whole. Where youth are visibly present in every aspect of congregational life, there the friendship of God is seen in a more egalitarian communion. Children and youth are friends of God who within the congregation become friends with members of every age. Mutual friendship between young people and their elders offers tangible evidence of God's kingdom in the company of the One who himself did not cast off but welcomed children (Mk 9:37).

Pastors, by virtue of their unique role as God's representatives, have the opportunity of welcoming others into the company of God. Whether it be on Sunday morning (before, during, or after worship) or at other times during the week (as one speaks to people in the office, over the phone, or on visits), the pastor's hospitality is a matter of great importance. Not only does it count in terms of how people evaluate a particular individual as pastor, but even more importantly, it makes an impact on how people perceive God. This is a tremendous responsibility but also an extraordinary opportunity. A pastor is invited into the crises of human life in a unique way. Being a pastor is both the best and worst of vocations for this very reason. For those so called, the satisfaction outweighs the burden.

In order to maintain perspective, there need to be supports that also sustain the pastor in God's friendship: caring relationships with other clergy, congregational support committees, regular participation in continuing education, good exercise habits, and a healthy prayer life. To lose one's own sense of divine friendship is to lose the very core of one's ministry. Should one reach a crisis in one's sense of calling, a pastor needs to be humble in reaching out for professional counseling, the very thing one would recommend to parishioners. What may at first appear as a devastating crisis may be transformed by the power of God into an occasion for identifying even more closely with the pain of others. Renewed by a vivid awareness of God's living presence through prayer, study, and collegial relationships, a pastor is able to serve as representative of God's friendship in the midst of a grateful people.

FOR FURTHER READING

Bonhoeffer, Dietrich. *Life Together/Prayerbook of the Bible.* Translated by Daniel W. Bloesch and James H. Burtness. Minneapolis: Fortress, 1996.

Fortune, Marie M. *Is Nothing Sacred? When Sex Invades the Pastoral Relationship.* San Francisco: Harper, 1992.

Friedman, Edward. *Generation to Generation: Family Process in Church and Synagogue.* New York: Guilford, 1985.

Hahn, Celia Allison. *Growing in Authority, Relinquishing Control: A New Approach to Faithful Leadership.* New York: The Alban Institute, 1994.

Kennedy, Eugene. *On Being a Friend.* New York: Continuum, 1982.

Olson, Mark A. *The Evangelical Pastor: Pastoral Leadership for a Witnessing People.* Minneapolis: Augsburg Fortress, 1992.

Palmer, Parker J. *The Company of Strangers: Christians and the Renewal of America's Public Life.* New York: Crossroad, 1981.

Peck, M. Scott. *The Different Drum: Community Making and Peace.* New York: Simon & Schuster, 1987.

Stone, Bryan P. *Compassionate Ministry: Theological Foundations.* Maryknoll: Orbis, 1996.

Whitehead, Evelyn Eaton, and Whitehead, James D. *Community of Faith: Crafting Christian Communities Today.* Mystic, Conn.: Twenty-Third Publications, 1993.

SEVEN

STEWARDSHIP: ALL THAT WE HAVE

Churches and Sunday schools in times past were accustomed to sing as the offering was collected: "We give thee but thine own, whate'er the gift may be; all that we have is thine alone, a trust, O Lord from thee." Today many congregations pray a prayer like this, following the offering of gifts: "We offer with joy and thanksgiving what you have first given us—our selves, our time, and our possessions, signs of your gracious love." In both cases something radical is uttered. The things that I claim to possess are not my own. Indeed the very life within me does not belong to me. All that I am and have are, when truly seen, gifts from God—God's possession, not my own.

The starting point for all Christian stewardship is the question of ownership. In liturgy we pretend to believe that God is the one who endows us with every gift, every possession, even the breath of life. Yet such an assertion runs against the grain of everything an acquisitive culture teaches us about the meaning and purpose of life. In this chapter we examine the question of ownership as the key issue in developing the theme of stewardship. Tithing is advocated as a means by which to begin to check one's idolatry. Lastly, the notion of "caring" is offered as a comprehensive rubric for interpreting the responsibility of the Christian life.

To understand oneself as steward grounds self-identity firmly in trusting God above all things. "Being in Christ," as formed through worship, shaped by Christian education, and nurtured in Christian fellowship, expands to become the orientation by which one views the entirety of one's life. Those who see themselves as "stewards of the mysteries of God" (1 Cor 4:1) may find themselves out of step with the prevailing order, structured on the accumulation of material possessions above all things. Instead of taking credit for one's own earnings, one lives in gratitude for God's bountiful goodness. Furthermore, one assumes responsibility that the world's goods be shared for the benefit of all, beginning with those most acutely in need.

OWNERSHIP

Legally speaking, we own many things. Our system of law has

detailed provisions for defining and defending the rights of private property. When purchasing a house, for example, the letter of the law must be followed in order to guarantee that the transaction is properly described and recorded in a way that will satisfy a court of law. Similarly, the title for an automobile is carefully monitored by the state. Even for minor purchases, one is wise to retain the sales slip to prove payment was made.

The system by which we earn wages, purchase items, save or invest money, and accumulate capital is pervasive. There exists a sense of general well-being when the stock market increases. Economic growth (GNP) becomes the primary measure by which we judge the success of a presidential administration. Self-worth is evaluated on the basis of net worth. A stigma is attached to the unemployed and welfare recipients, those who do not or cannot produce. Advertising looms on every possible horizon, beckoning us to see our primary identity according to what we consume.

Theologically speaking, however, we own nothing. "The earth is the LORD's and all that is in it, the world, and those who live in it" (Ps 24:1). What we dare to confess liturgically is that God is the owner of the entire world; this includes my life, time, energy, and property, together with those of every person on earth. To God as creator and sustainer of all things we owe our gratitude and thanksgiving for what we have, provisions from God's own hand.

In the ministry of Jesus and the earliest church we see evidence of this theological understanding of ownership. Jesus tells his disciples to travel lightly, taking nothing for the journey except a staff (symbol of itinerancy); no bread, no bag, no money in their belts, not even a change of clothes. The disciples were to depend upon the hospitality of others for their maintenance, returning the good news of the kingdom (Mk 6:7-13). Similarly, the church of Jerusalem is remembered in Acts for the practice of sharing: "No one claimed private ownership of any possessions, but everything they owned was held in common" (4:32b). This is not to say that there were no Christians who held substantial wealth. But it does raise the question on whose behalf one administers one's possessions.

The essential meaning of stewardship is that the steward holds and administers a property on behalf of another. The steward is held responsible for neither squandering nor mismanaging what belongs to another. In every case, however, it is clear that the steward is not the owner but the responsible agent taking care of a possession precious to the superior. This symbol, taken from economic practices of the ancient world, speaks powerfully regarding our proper attitude to property as well. Theologically speaking, God is the owner and we are stewards, answerable to the owner for our management of what does not belong to us.

The contrast between this theological understanding of possessions and the prevalent legal approach that dominates our culture creates a profound dissonance for those who belong to Christ. It means that Christians live in an acute tension with the values of the culture that surrounds them. The constant temptation is to rationalize according to the common norms of earning, acquisition, consumption, and ownership. To abandon such measures of worth is to commit an act of heresy against the ruling orthodoxy of economics and the good life. There exists no easy resolution of this dilemma. Still today, one cannot serve God and mammon at the same time (Lk 16:13).

To assume the role of a steward with relationship to the things of the world is to reorient the entirety of one's outlook. The ultimate source of my security is not located in earning capacity, savings accounts, investments, or insurance policies. Like the birds of the air and the lilies of the field, the final source of my security rests in the hands of a benevolently providing God (Mt 6:25-33). Anxiety over food and clothing is wasted. Rather, keeping one's eye on the kingdom supplants all other concerns. Such an attitude is perceived as infinitely impractical and even subversive of the status quo. This may be true. It also sounds like an excuse for sloth. Yet this it is not.

The steward, viewing the things of the earth not as one's own, turns eyes away from preoccupation with the self to see the pressing needs of the neighbor. What replaces my self-concern is genuine concern for the other. No longer is the belief permissible that each individual's selfish striving will miraculously work out for the benefit of all. Rather, the priority of the steward is responsiveness to those most in need, the least of the brothers and sisters (Mt 25:31-46). In our age of ecological devastation, this includes responsiveness to the needs of the earth itself. Indeed, the requirement of the steward is to advocate a preferential option for the poor—the homeless, the hungry, the powerless, and the very ecosphere that sustains us all. The steward undertakes such advocacy not for the sake of some political agenda but as an integral aspect of kingdom responsibility, the kingdom belonging to God.

The energy once directed toward self-enhancement and self-promotion does not dissipate. By the power of the Spirit and in the company of Christian fellowship, that energy is instead redirected. Within the established system, this means that I continue to work diligently but now as one answerable to the authority of God. My self-worth does not come from the amount I am able to accumulate—that is, the one with the most toys does not "win"—but derives from my faith in the gracious love of the God who created me and all that exists. The profit from my labors becomes the capital that I administer as a steward on behalf of the one who provided it. The overriding concern in the management of the portion of God's bounty assigned to me is how to employ this wealth on behalf of others, especially those most in need. What better motivation for diligent and responsible employment could one imagine! Yet the entire enterprise shifts from an egocentric to a theocentric perspective.

Stewardship can never become an all-encompassing approach to life until we liberate it from the ghetto of annual campaigns to balance congregational budgets. Such campaigns may well be a necessary function of church life, especially given our present method of operation. But stewardship means far more, that is, the surrender of all that I have to God and God alone.

TITHING: A CHECK ON IDOLATRY

Those who take seriously the call to view their livelihood and goods as God's possession may find themselves in a quandary. First, there is the issue of guilt. How does one appease one's guilt for the plenty that is enjoyed when the world is marked by such radical disparity between "haves" and "have nots"? The law of fairness and equity requires disquietude as one perceives how many are those who suffer daily in want.

Yet the gospel will not allow us to remain paralyzed by our guilt, whether it be prompted by what we have done or what we have left undone. Instead the gospel of Jesus Christ sets us free from being frozen by the magnitude of the world's problems to function within the realm of responsibility afforded to us. God's steward manages the assigned property with skill and responsibility regardless of how others manage the lot assigned to them. Faithfulness to the charge of the owner is the steward's chief aim, not success in eradicating seemingly intractable problems on a grand scale. A steward takes charge with the freedom of one who knows the grace and forgiveness of God in Jesus Christ.

A second aspect of the dilemma facing the steward is the discrepancy between the economic values of the world and those of the kingdom. The tension between a life lived by the standard of accumulation and the kingdom's norm of sharing is extreme. In order to survive as a steward, one will need to return often to the sanctuary. There one's identity as a citizen of the kingdom becomes renewed. Within the fellowship of the church, one discovers encouragement for swimming against the culture's stream of acquisitiveness and consumption.

A third question is where to begin. Especially with regard to financial affairs, this is a delicate matter. There is one obvious reason why it is so terribly difficult to speak about money in the church: when we talk about money we touch that which is God's real rival for our allegiance. In this society it is money that serves as our greatest idol. While we mock ancient peoples for their ignorance in "worshiping" statues, we fail to acknowledge the idolatry inherent in our attitude toward the almighty dollar. As the writing on the bill announces, "In God we trust." In this culture, life revolves around maximization of economic advantage. Generations from now, archaeologists will discern that the greatest monuments of this age were not cathedrals but shopping malls. What does this testify about us?

One place to begin if one is serious about stewardship is with the tithe. While tithing is an ancient practice whose roots can be traced to the law codes of Israel, it is not the purpose here to justify tithing with proof texts. If anything, Jesus' criticism of the Pharisees for their perfunctory tithing ought to make us wary of the practice (Mt 23:23). Instead, tithing will here be advocated as a reasonable and realizable first step in checking our impulse toward the idolatry of money.

Tithing ought never be imposed as a requirement. The danger of a legalistic approach is real. God's love is free and merciful. God makes the sun to shine and rain to fall on all without discrimination. Tithing will not assist one to receive a special blessing from God. Tithing does not make one a better Christian than someone else who does not.

The reason to consider the tithe is for the sake of organizing an assault on one's idolatry of money. If God is indeed the owner of all that has been apportioned to me, then my only proper response is thanksgiving and gratitude for all God has provided. This certainly includes my time and talents but also my financial resources. To God belongs not just 10 percent but the entire 100 percent of what I have. In order to begin to loosen the vice grip that money has on our lives, however, one chooses to commit to the tithe as a symbol of intent. It is as if one says, "I intend to direct my loyalty and pledge my allegiance to God above all things. As a token of this commitment, I offer a tithe of my income to the work of the kingdom."

Some might choose to gradually adjust to this level of giving. Others might decide to take an abrupt plunge. Still others might in time move well beyond ten percent to larger amounts. There is a sense in which the ability to give is a charism that differs among us. The final purpose of tithing is not how much one gives but the attitude of gratefulness to God. The aim is to establish worship of God as the highest priority. Tithing is an aid to setting one's financial house in order, rendering to God the things that are God's, that is, everything one is and has (Mk 12:17).

One consequence of the widespread practice of tithing in the church would be to make available enormous sums of money for the sake of mission. This money would enhance not only the work of local congregations but global mission, new congregations domestically, hunger programs, and a variety of forms of service to humanity. The resources derived from the tithe need not be directed only to the church but could be offered for other charitable causes as well.

While advocacy of tithing may stir up objections of many kinds, the fundamental issue that it addresses in our time is that of idolatry. Joshua once issued the challenge to the people of Israel: "Choose this day whom you will serve, whether the gods your ancestors served in the region beyond the River or the gods of the Amorites in whose land you are living" (Jos 24:15). Tithing is one way we today might answer with Joshua: "As for me and my household, we will serve the LORD."

CARING

"We care because God first cared for us" (cf. 1 Jn 4:19). Translating the Greek word *agápe* as "care" instead of "love" discloses dimensions of meaning easily lost in a culture where talk of "love" is cheap. God's love for us does not come cheaply. Its fullest expression comes in the person of Jesus whose relationships to others were marked by care and whose death on the cross provides evidence of the ultimate act of caring, to lay down one's life for another. As we discuss stewardship as a matter of caring, we do so in acknowledgment that God is the paradigmatic caregiver who cares for us in order that we might care for others.

In his beautiful book, *On Caring,* Milton Mayeroff describes the purpose of caring as providing for the growth and development of another person. Caring is not performed as an act of manipulation. It does not occur for the satisfaction of one's own unmet needs. Rather, caring transpires for the sake of the other's own genuine need to become whole and to grow as a person. In adapting Mayeroff's definition of caring to Christian thinking, the aim of caring becomes attending to another so that this one too is capacitated to function as a person who cares. The goal of growth is not just understood as a means of self-actualization but becomes the manner by which a kingdom of caring is extended in the world. Caring begets caring. God's care for us enables our care for one another and for the world. We care for others with God's care to that they too become people who care.

As God's stewards, we are summoned to learn a life of caring. A congregation is a community that fosters caring. Such care begins with respect for oneself. While there is too much talk these days about "doing something just for yourself," one cannot begin to care for others until one is both free from preoccupation with one's own needs and energized to attend to the other. The ultimate form of self-care, from a Christian perspective, is trusting in the promise of God's personal love. Unless one's life is rooted in God's unconditional care, the foundation of caring for others is tenuous. This means that self-care not only entails attention to diet, sleep, and exercise as essential components but also necessarily includes prayer, devotions, and worship. As one is regularly cared for by the Word and Sacraments of God, one receives a centered focus that sets one free to care for others.

The primary laboratory in which one learns the requisites of caring is the family. If one is to acquire the habit of caring, then one must begin with the practice of listening, patience, forbearance, courage, self-sacrifice, trust, and forgiveness as it unfolds in the life of a family.

Whether it be the relationships with parents, siblings, spouse, or children, the intense closeness of a family challenges every idealistic portrait of human community. Family life provides the arena in which the most destructive of human behaviors can emerge. And at the same time, families offer a glimpse of what human community was intended to be. What one learns about caring from one's own family of origin serves as the basis for one's ability to care in the world beyond one's family. A successful family nurtures individuals who themselves are capacitated to move beyond its boundary into relationships of care for others.

The circle of care extends into the realms of the congregation, workplace, and local community. The congregation at worship provides a locale where one practices the rudiments of caring, as already described. The relationships among members of a congregation provide ample opportunity to exercise care, whether its expression be listening or doing a favor. Projects of the congregation offer various outlets where care for those in special need can be organized and executed.

The workplace too is a setting in which one has regular opportunity for rendering care. This takes place initially through the responsible fulfillment of vocational duties. Luther liked to describe the workplace as the arena through which God upholds the fabric of creation. If one cares, that will be evident in one's attitude toward one's job. Those who experience a lack of meaningful employment require counseling either to discover ways to renew their sense of purpose or to risk setting out in a new direction. With the precariousness of the current employment situation, many feel trapped in unfulfilling work due to their need for an income. Yet it may be a greater tragedy to pour out one's lifeblood in an occupation that one detests solely for the sake of a paycheck than to risk a change.

The workplace also affords the opportunity to care for the persons with whom one works. A level of familiarity is attained among colleagues at work that affords the possibility of genuine caring. A steward, nurtured in the experience of Christian community in the congregation, has a model for relating to others that goes beyond business as usual. Expressions of solidarity in the joys and sorrows of those one knows at work extends the arena of God's caring in powerful ways.

A steward sees not only the realms of church, family, and work as avenues for caring but also the wider community. Schools, civic organizations, charitable causes, and volunteer groups each offer possible arenas of service. For some there is the danger of making too many commitments and therefore not being able to do any of them well. For most Christians, however, there is too little thought given to service in the community as a kind of stewardship. One ought even to recognize one's involvement in the political process as an extension of Christian stewardship, as we care collectively for the leadership and direction of our community's common life.

The service area of Christian stewardship and caring goes beyond all the circles already mentioned, however, to encompass the entire globe. Issues confronting the nation—health care, criminal justice, domestic violence, and so forth—summon a thoughtful response from Christians who care. Likewise the affairs of other nations raise questions of responsibility for the steward—war, hunger, terrorism, and so on. It has in our time become especially urgent to develop a conscientious policy of caring for the earth and its endangered ecosystems. Each of these matters we will take up again in remaining chapters.

The congregation, by instilling the mindset of stewardship within its membership and by corporately practicing the art of caring, reinforces a strong sense of Christian identity. The church, composed of its many members, is accountable to God for taking care of the portion assigned to it for safekeeping. The idea of stewardship grounds congregational identity in its relationship and responsibility to God above all else. At the same time, the matter of stewardship points the congregation beyond itself to the mission of caring for the earth and all that dwell therein. Within a theology of the congregation, stewardship functions at the juncture between concern for identity and activation in mission.

The previous four chapters have elaborated the first of two foci in a theology of the congregation. Worship, education, fellowship, and stewardship are indispensable components of a congregation that knows its true identity. At worship congregation rehearses its identity as people of the kingdom. There it meets its living Lord in Word and Sacrament, who transforms it into the people of God whom by its own power it can only pretend to be. A congregation immerses itself in the way of Christian discipleship through its educational efforts, following the example of the saints who have gone before. The congregation celebrates the friendship of God in Christ through its "life together" (Bonhoeffer) in egalitarian communion—people and pastor, those of every age, color, and social position. Within the congregation, the people of God learn to see themselves as stewards of all God has given them. Tithing and caring, they express their gratitude.

In worship, education, fellowship, and stewardship, a congregation knows its identity as a people gathered in the name of Jesus Christ. Whenever a congregation begins to forget the One who is its origin, it must return again to these basic elements. Yet the purpose of the congregation transcends the formation of identity. The same Jesus who calls us together also sends us out to the world in mission. For this reason we next take up four components that accent the congregation's essential mission: evangelism, global connections, ecumenism, and social ministry. Without these expressions of outreach, the vitality of the church begins to atrophy and wither.

FOR FURTHER READING

Brown, L. David. *Take Care: A Guide for Responsible Living.* Minneapolis: Augsburg, 1978.

Cunningham, Richard B. *Creative Stewardship.* Nashville: Abingdon, 1989.

Fischer, Wallace E. *All Good Gifts: On Doing Biblical Stewardship.* Minneapolis: Augsburg, 1979.

Gifford, Hartland H. *All That God Has Given: Faithful Stewardship as Followers of Jesus.* Minneapolis: Augsburg, 1993.

Hall, Douglas J. *The Steward: A Biblical Symbol Come to Age.* Grand Rapids: Eerdmans, 1989.

Heyd, Thomas. *Planning for Stewardship: Developing a Giving Program for Congregations.* Minneapolis: Augsburg, 1980.

Johnson, Douglas W. *The Tithe: Challenge or Legalism?* Nashville: Abingdon, 1989.

Mayeroff, Milton. *On Caring.* New York: Harper & Row, 1971.

Meeks, M. Douglas. *God the Economist: The Doctrine of God and Political Economy.* Minneapolis: Fortress, 1989.

Westerhoff, John H. III. *Building God's People in a Materialistic Society.* San Francisco: Harper & Row, 1983.

PART THREE

MISSION

INTRODUCTION TO PART THREE

A holistic theology of the congregation revolves around two poles, identity and mission. In part two we examined the ministry of the congregation with an eye toward those functions that most contribute to the formation and nurture of Christian identity: worship, education, fellowship, and stewardship. Already the tone of the discussion has pointed, however, toward the movement of congregational ministry from focus on its identity to outreach in mission. The mission of the congregation to be addressed in the next four chapters is also organized under four categories: evangelism, global connections, ecumenism, and social ministry. Together these dimensions of mission provide direction for a comprehensive vision of congregational interaction with a local community and the world at large.

We might again ask at this juncture: "What is the purpose of the Christian congregation?" The answer that guides these chapters is this: "The purpose of the Christian congregation is to be a mediator of the salvation that God in Jesus Christ is bringing to all people." By "salvation" is meant *God's* project of bringing wholeness to human life by restoring us to right relationships—with God, neighbor, and the creation itself. The gospel of salvation is proclaimed as the forgiveness of sins and the justification of the sinner before God, inviting the individual into a living relationship with God based on trust. The meaning of salvation, however, also transcends individual piety to incorporate the complex web of human relationships with one another and the created world.

Evangelism focuses on the task of proclaiming the gospel to individuals and families in order that they might be incorporated into the people of God, the church. Salvation becomes personal through the work of congregations that are evangelical. Global connections establish the breadth of God's salvific concern, a concern that relativizes national boundaries and distinctions in favor of one, holy, catholic, and apostolic church on earth. This dimension of the congregation's life achieves new importance in an age of mass communication when our mutual interdependence becomes increasingly obvious. Ecumenism broadens the scope of the congregation's mission to include the restoration of relationships among Christians, who have been divided into hundreds of denominations and sects. Salvation occurs as estranged Christian groups move toward fellowship at the Lord's table.

Finally, social ministry, for example, among the hungry and those threatened by violence and on behalf of an endangered earth's ecosystem, aims to reestablish relationships in accordance with the church's vision of the kingdom of God. The mission of God, in whose service the church seeks to minister, finds its final consummation in the eternity of God's eschatological kingdom. In the meantime, the church properly serves God's salvific purposes by engaging in diverse ministries that aim at a more just structuring of power relationships and the resolution of conflict by peaceful means.

The mission of the church, and thereby the congregation, is not an either/or concentration—either on individuals or on social problems. Rather, the salvation of God intends integrally incorporates both dimensions. A congregation's mission is diminished to the degree that it fails to include in some measure all four of the aspects now to be elaborated.

EIGHT

EVANGELISM: TELLING THE KINGDOM

"Thank the Lord and sing God's praise! Tell everyone what God has done!"

S o begins a familiar liturgical hymn that points to the core impulse of evangelism. Recalling a favorite revival hymn, "I love to tell the story of Jesus and his love," again we are reminded that good news deserves telling. Whether it be the good news of a birth, a graduation, a promotion, or a recent trip, it is intrinsic to human nature to share good news with others. Even stronger then should be the drive to share the best of all news: the message of Jesus, the kingdom, forgiveness of sins, the power of the cross, friendship with God, and eternal life.

While there are certain basic techniques of communication that congregational evangelists do well to master, the danger is that we have turned evangelism into something imposing and difficult, something that must be carefully studied and therefore best left to trained professionals. It is essential that members of congregations return to some basic principles of evangelism and then simply open their mouths to share what they have heard. Worship that gives prominence to the Scriptures and the preached word is inherently evangelical. On a weekly basis, the proclaimed gospel extends and deepens the lifelong process of conversion among the gathered congregation. The experience of worship becomes a central basis for congregation members to talk about how God has met them in their lives as they invite others also to "come and see" (Jn 1:46).

BACK TO THE BASICS

Mention of the word "evangelism" leaves many tongue-tied and virtually paralyzed. We are afraid of being stereotyped as religious fanatics and offending another's sensibilities. The conviction has grown in the church that evangelism is something complicated and hard to comprehend. Therefore we tend to organize classes to learn about evangelism. We study and we study and we study evangelism, nearly to death. Deep inside we develop the belief that only someone thoroughly trained can do the work of an evangelist. We prefer to leave the task to the trained professionals and to the clergy. Frequently a few members take on the thankless task of "doing evangelism" on behalf of the rest. And the gospel fails to be told as it should because members are afraid to open their lips.

When it comes to the work of evangelism, congregations need to return to some very basic notions and simply go out to spread the word. In contrast to the risk facing the disciples of Jesus, the risks we face are minor. Mark 6:7-13 recounts the first missionary journey of the twelve. Recalling the basic instructions of Jesus to these evangelists can assist us to rediscover our bearings for the task set before us. This brief text sets forth four guidelines that continue to remain relevant in our vastly different context.

First, Jesus extends to the twelve his own authority, the authority of the kingdom of God. They are given power over unclean spirits and ability to heal. They proceed as those who speak in Jesus' stead and in Jesus' name. There is a boldness with which they are commissioned. While today we might go forth as evangelists with less anticipation of serving as agents of God's miraculous healing power, we do well to recall that when we speak to others about our faith, we do so not for our own sake but for the sake of the gospel. The spirit of Jesus will be present to uphold and sustain our work. And the spirit of Jesus comes alive through what we say. Wherever Jesus is present, there healing occurs, if not physical then inward and spiritual. This first guideline grounds our task in the mission of Jesus, not in ourselves. This lends a measure of audacity to our efforts as evangelists, needed today in a time when many are embarrassed by their Christian faith.

Second, the disciples are sent out in pairs and return to share their experiences from the mission front. There is wisdom in visiting others in pairs where possible. In the company of another there is the basis for mutual support before, during, and after an encounter. Visiting in teams buoys confidence as one takes the difficult initiative in reaching out. We can depend on the words of a partner when our own words falter in a conversation. And we can reflect together on the visit upon departure.

Third, we go forth to tell the news unencumbered, both of material attachments and of status. For the first disciples, the lifestyle was spartan. Jesus instructed them to take no bread, no bag, no money, no change of clothes. They were to wear sandals and carry only a staff, signs of their itinerancy. They were to keep moving from village to village, depending on the hospitality of those who might welcome them. In this fashion they not only were devoid of material security but also lacked a position of status in society. They were totally dependent on the mercy of those whom they visited.

Is it not exactly our encumbrances that prevent us from going forth to tell the good news to others? Like Martha in the Gospel of Luke, we are "worried and distracted by many things" (10:41). Telephone calls, automobile repairs, errands, children's schedules, pet care, banking, committee meetings at church, and so forth—our days are full of what "must" be accomplished. Modern conveniences and a multitude of commitments eat up the minutes and hours and days of our lives. The good life leaves no time for "the better part" (Lk 10:42).

Also we are encumbered by the status we have achieved. No less than in biblical times, we work long and hard to establish our place in society. While we admit to being Christian, we also know there is a special niche in the social scale for those who talk too much about Jesus. So out of fear of losing status in the eyes of others, we remain silent. We are encumbered by appearances and are afraid to fall to a lower rung on the ladder of social opinion. Before we can move freely as witnesses to the gospel, we need to become less encumbered by many good things and less impeded by the opinion of others. Is there not a way to say the gospel of Jesus with integrity and genuine concern for another that does not require my shame and their guilt?

Lastly, the disciples were dependent on the hospitality of whoever might welcome them. While we would prefer to imagine that they proceeded triumphantly, welcomed at every door, the text suggests otherwise. There are clear instructions for what to do when a place refuses to welcome and receive them. Who knows if this did not occur often?

For us this serves as a reminder that any hospitality that comes to us as messengers of the gospel is a gift. We should not necessarily expect to be well received. In fact, we might expect rejection to be frequent. When welcomed, as good guests we must be gracious in receiving what the host has to offer. This includes carefully listening to the stories that might be shared. We do so reserving judgment. The gospel word, we trust, has something to offer every circumstance of life. We seek to tailor its impact to fit what we hear from those who welcome us. Good guests, the text instructs, also know when it is time to depart.

While the circumstances separating us from these first disciples are vastly different, the lessons to be learned for the art of evangelism are timeless. The gospel remains fresh to all who will hear: God is not far away but near, not condemning but merciful; Jesus died on the cross to reveal the infinity of God's forgiveness and love; this Jesus yet lives as a spiritual presence to guide one's individual journey through life; God's kingdom aims at the salvific reordering of human relationships; beyond death awaits eternal life in God's heaven. This gospel is something each member of every congregation already knows from hearing "the old, old story" time and time again. There are few if any new techniques to master. The only obstacle that prevents congregations from engaging in active evangelism is inertia. And the place where that inertia is overcome is in worship.

WEEKLY CONVERSION

Churches in the revival tradition culminate worship services with an altar call. Those desiring to publicly profess their conversion to Christian faith do so by coming forward to the front of the church. Converts know and remember the time, date, and place when they accepted Jesus as Lord and Savior. They learn to witness to others by detailing how they sinned before coming to Christ, how their hearts were changed by hearing the gospel, and how their lives have been different since conversion.

Liturgical churches have something valuable to learn from this practice. While theologically it would be wrong for them to introduce an altar call into the order for worship (given the priority of God's grace over human decision in the act of conversion), the significance of our worship could be enhanced by deeper reflection on the nature of conversion as an ongoing process in the life of the worshiper. Properly understood, we become Christians only once and that by virtue of our baptism into Christ. Yet our conversion to discipleship does not occur so suddenly. Rather, conversion to discipleship takes place over the course of a lifetime.

One of the strongest arguments for regular weekly participation in worship is that each Christian is involved in an ongoing process of conversion. Sunday worship serves as a time for "weekly conversion" to Christian discipleship. As we journey through life, there arise ever new challenges and dilemmas. Our Christian faith is a resource for helping us face each new turn. Worship so immerses us in the way of Jesus that we discover new angles from which to examine our problems. Within the fellowship of the congregation, we discover friends who support us as we struggle with difficult decisions. In the proclamation of the gospel and at the communion table we receive grace for when we falter, forgiveness for our sin.

Worship, as the occasion for weekly conversion to the person and way of Jesus, serves as the time when the evangelists are evangelized. According to this line of thought, nonbelievers are not the only ones in need of evangelism. Instead, the evangel needs to be heard over and over again, on a weekly basis where possible, also by the baptized. Ever new shadows appear requiring the light of the gospel. Ever new dilemmas arise to challenge Christian faith and practice. Our understanding of evangelism must be broad enough to include the continuing evangelization of the baptized and specific enough to focus on evangelical outreach to those outside the Christian community. Worship that establishes Word and Sacrament at the center—Bible-oriented proclamation and regular celebration of Baptism and Eucharist—is evangelical in both senses. Regular worshipers are repeatedly converted to the central importance of the gospel for their lives. Visitors and inquirers perceive that here is something worth living for. Worship services need not be transformed into hours of entertainment. The congregation that gathers to pretend and become the kingdom of God will testify powerfully to the reality and truth of the gospel in their midst. By so doing they are inherently evangelical and evangelistic. Worship as a time of weekly conversion serves as the central focus for all the congregation's evangelism efforts.

LITURGY AS A PRIMER FOR WITNESS

Where does a congregation turn for direction in developing the evangelical impulse as an expression of its life together? Often the tendency is to turn to those traditions that have already developed "successful" evangelism programs, success being measured primarily by the standard of numerical growth. With minimal theological reflection, congregations adopt the approach and tactics of the four spiritual laws, church growth, or the Evangelism Explosion program. When these or similar programs are uncritically adopted, however, one fails to recognize the theological option that is also implicitly made. These approaches emphasize the element of faith decision on the part of the individual at the expense of attributing faith to the work of God's Spirit. Conversion tends to become a matter of self-achievement, accomplished once in the past at a certain place and time.

How different from this is the understanding of evangelism set forth in Article 5 of the Augsburg Confession: "In order that we may obtain this faith, the ministry of teaching the Gospel and administering the sacraments was instituted. For through the Word and the sacraments, as through instruments, the Holy Spirit is given, and the Holy Spirit produces faith, where and when it pleases God, in those who hear the Gospel." This assertion challenges us to totally rethink our orientation as we undertake evangelism in the congregation. The starting point for evangelism shifts away from the isolated experience of an individual to the living center of congregational life, worship.

While we profess that it is in Word and Sacrament that God in Christ meets us in our lives, how does this conviction alter our approach to evangelism? Instead of encouraging members to develop a testimony based on a decisionist model of conversion, as many do, the experience of participation in liturgical worship opens a new avenue. Education for evangelism becomes assisting people to become articulate about how God has ministered to them through Word and Sacrament within the context of the liturgy. If we believe that God in Christ is truly present in our gathering for worship, then this experience becomes a rich reservoir from which to draw in learning to tell others the good news.

Insofar as shyness is the issue that blocks evangelism, the liturgy serves as a primer for guiding us to speak. Members can first be encouraged to consider the ways in which God has ministered to them at worship. Moments of crisis and times of transition are frequently recalled as occasions when God spoke in a powerful way through the media of Word and Sacrament. One might remember how at a time of guilt or despair, the declaration of forgiveness lifted a tremendous burden. Or one might acknowledge that the regular ritual of confession and absolution offers a necessary weekly reminder of a fresh start with God. Another might learn to talk about a time of joy when a particular hymn of praise gave expression to one's sense of gratitude. References to favorite hymns offer the opportunity to talk about both a hymn's content and the special meaning it bears.

With reference to the Scripture, one might talk about the significance that particular Bible stories have borne at various junctures of life. One might detail the impact made by a certain sermon preached at the time one was searching for an answer. Perhaps one even tells of a time when a sermon presented a challenge to reassess and revise a dearly beloved prejudice. Witnessing to the power of sermons as the living voice of God through the words of the preacher stimulates the expectancy of others for what happens in preaching.

When one wavers in one's faith, it might be appropriate to explain the reassurance one gains from confessing the creed, as the faith of others carries us along through periods of doubt. The prayers of the church can be a point of reference for describing how God through prayer ministered at a time of personal illness or the sickness of a loved one.

One's participation in the sacraments also lends a basis for talking about one's faith. The promises of God to love, forgive, and extend eternal salvation are made personal in baptism. One can talk either about the meaning of one's own baptism or describe the occasion of the baptism of another. Similarly, one can testify to the presence of Christ in the sacrament of Holy Communion and speak personally of the grace received, especially with reference to particular moments when the sacrament took on additional meaning, for example, at the time of a death.

Those who follow a liturgical order of worship have a wealth of experiences to employ in their evangelical outreach. The challenge is for us to learn to speak confidently about what we already know to be God's encounter with us in worship. In approaching evangelism from the orientation of worship, two goals are accomplished. First, we have the opportunity of speaking in an authentic way about our own experience of God made manifest in worship. Thus is avoided the temptation of borrowing from a tradition that is foreign from our common experience of God's activity through liturgy. Second, we invite others to discover Christ in the place he promises to be found, that is, Word and Sacrament. There are good reasons to invite people to worship. It's not a matter of making God happy by "going to church." Rather, worship is the place where God in Christ promises to minister to the needs of those who gather. We invite others so they too might discover what we have found. In the words of Luther, evangelism is one beggar telling another beggar where to find bread. Or it is the simple witness of a Philip who says to his skeptical brother, "Come and see" (Jn 1:46).

FOR FURTHER READING

Armstrong, Richard Stoll. *The Pastor as Evangelist.* Philadelphia: Westminster, 1984.

Callahan, Kenneth L. *Visiting in the Age of Mission: A Handbook for Person-to-Person Ministry.* San Francisco: Harper, 1994.

Hunter III, George G. *How to Reach Secular People.* Nashville: Abingdon, 1992.

Johnson, Ben. *An Evangelism Primer: Practical Principles for Congregations.* Atlanta: John Knox, 1983.

Keifert, Patrick R. *Welcoming the Stranger: A Public Theology of Worship and Evangelism.* Minneapolis: Fortress, 1992.

Krass, Alfred C. *Evangelizing Neopagan North America.* Scottdale, Pa.: Herald, 1982.

Quere, Ralph W. *Evangelical Witness: The Message, Medium, Mission, and Method of Evangelism.* Minneapolis: Augsburg, 1975.

Schmalenberger, Jerry L. *Called To Witness: A Manual for Congregational Growth.* Lima, Ohio: C.S.S. Publishing, 1993.

Senn, Frank C. *The Witness of the Worshipping Community: Liturgy and the Practice of Evangelism.* New York and Mahwah, N.J.: Paulist, 1993.

NINE

GLOBAL CONNECTIONS: THE CHURCH CATHOLIC

"We believe in one holy catholic and apostolic church."

The church has confessed this faith since the fourth century in the words of the Nicene Creed. Following the Reformation and the ensuing polemic between Protestants and Roman Catholics, many Protestant groups changed the translation of the word "catholic" to "Christian." While an understandable change given the animosity generated over centuries of mistrust, we can rejoice that the confessional climate has improved to the point where we can return to the use of the original word and its original meaning. Catholic means universal. We confess at worship by means of this creed that God rules over one, single, universal church, a church undivided over time and space. Throughout history and today throughout the world, in God's eyes there exists only one catholic church.

Clearly this is a confession of faith, not a statement based on empirical evidence. The church of Jesus Christ appears fragmented into groupings based on nationality, language, race, and many other characteristics. Yet, as we confess in this creed, that which divides us does not constitute the essence of the church God intends. Rather, as there is only one Lord, one faith, and one baptism (Eph 4:5), so there exists in reality only one catholic church. The one great obstacle to this confession is that we do not live as though it were true.

Christian congregations are called by the Holy Spirit to live in the reality of the one catholic church that we confess. There are numerous ways that individual congregations can express their connectedness to Christians and churches in other parts of the world. This chapter explores the imperative that every congregation develop global connections that give expression to the breadth of the faith we confess. Christians in other parts of the world desperately need us to subordinate the rhetoric of nationalism to the unity we share in Christ. By baptism we have been formed into one body. When our brothers and sisters on other continents are in pain, we too suffer with them. Likewise, when they rejoice, we receive great blessings. "Let us pray for the *whole* people of God in

Christ Jesus and for *all* people according to their needs" (*Lutheran Book of Worship*, 65).

CENTRIFUGAL FORCE OF THE GOSPEL

The catholicity of the church of Jesus Christ came clearly to expression already on Pentecost, the church's birthday. The Holy Spirit in wind and flame united in faith those whose languages and nationalities otherwise would serve to divide. Each one heard the others speaking in the native language of each (Acts 2:6). While skeptics sneered, the Holy Spirit revealed the catholicity of the church that relativized the barriers of language, race, and nationality conventionally used to carve up humanity. The Holy Spirit enlivened human understanding to unite all those gathered into the one catholic church of Jesus Christ.

The spirit of Pentecost propelled the apostles outward. The gospel of the resurrected Jesus contains a centrifugal force that thrust these members of the earliest church into a universal mission. Though themselves Jews by birth and circumcision, the apostles were entrusted with the commission to baptize all who repented and believed the good news. Not without agony did the Jerusalem church concede that Gentiles be admitted as equal partners in the church without the necessity of submitting to at least some provisions of the Law. As Acts tells the story, however, under the persistent challenge of a Paul and the persuasion of the Spirit over a Peter, Gentiles came to belong to the church of Jesus Christ by their confession of faith alone.

In the early decades after the resurrection, the gospel of Jesus Christ spread with amazing celerity. Using the privilege of Roman citizenship and his upbringing as a Pharisee, Paul took the gospel first to Jews and then to Gentiles throughout the southern reaches of the Roman empire. Soon there were followers of the Way of Jesus Christ not only in Palestine and Syria but also in Cappadocia, Galatia, Asia Minor, Macedonia, and even Rome itself. The common experience of persecution and even martyrdom demonstrates that these early Christians understood the catholicity of the church. Many willingly suffered humiliation and death rather than submit to the machinations of an empire requiring them to confess the divinity of Caesar. The blood of the martyrs bound the followers of Jesus in a community that transcended all other allegiances.

The Romanization of the church, set in motion when Constantine bestowed favored status upon the church beginning in the fourth century, gave new meaning to the word "catholic." As the empire convulsed to the breaking point, one political aim of the emperor was to employ Christianity as a cement to bind together what was ripping apart. The formulation of the Nicene Creed itself was influenced by these developments as the political order looked to the church to provide a basis for unity. This led to the development of Christendom, outlined in chapter five, which compromised the integrity of Christian conviction.

At the same time, the Constantinian arrangement gave the church institutional advantages for spreading the word about Jesus to the farthest reaches of Rome's influence. During the Holy Roman empire, converts to Jesus from the British isles took the gospel in the fifth, sixth, and seventh centuries into the remainder of western Europe. From 800 to 1300, the process of Christianization spread northward into Scandinavia and eastward across eastern Europe. In the years after 1400, Christian mission extended itself ever farther eastward toward Asia.

The close connection between baptism and citizenship in the church of the Middle Ages was a blessing for facilitating access to new territory but a curse in terms of compromising the content of the faith. The significance of baptism as that which constitutes the catholicity of the church became subordinate to the exigencies of good citizenship. This confusion about Christian identity is nowhere more manifest than in the struggles of the Reformation of the sixteenth century. What constitutes true Christianity? Submission to the dictates of the Holy Roman Emperor? Submission to the decrees of the Holy Roman Pope? Or submission to the Lordship of Jesus Christ as revealed in Holy Scripture? The Reformation gave the occasion for decoupling baptism from citizenship. Ironically, this moment of opportunity gave rise not so much to greater loyalty to Jesus Christ that transcended the boundaries dividing countries, but rather to a new and more avid territorialism. Churches became ever more closely identified with political rule under the provisions of the Peace of Westphalia (1648), whereby the religion of the territorial ruler determined the favored religion of the territory.

During the age of European expansion, Christianity spread through missionary efforts and immigration to both North and South America. Tragically this was a period in which the gospel message was too regularly used as an imperialistic weapon, lending deep ambiguity to the evangelization process. The nineteenth century saw the apex of organized missionary activity to Africa and Asia. Again a tragic dimension permeated this period as the Christian gospel was too narrowly identified with Western culture. It has only been in recent decades that the church has begun to intentionally divest the Christian message of its cultural bias in order to think Christian truth with integrity in ways indigenous to host cultures.

This all too cursory survey of the globalization of Christianity aims to demonstrate that the thrust of the gospel is inherently inclusive of all people on earth, regardless of language, race, or nationality. Unlike other world religions (with the exception of Islam), Christianity is inherently a missionary religion that aims at unifying all humankind by faith in Christ Jesus. Baptism is no respecter of human distinctions, but theologically acts as the mechanism that creates a new community, uniting persons in the body of Christ as a form of community that makes all other allegiances subordinate. Jesus Christ died for all. And so by faith in Jesus Christ all are joined into a new fellowship that relativizes all other human bonds. Under the parenthood of God, Jesus taught that all his followers are sisters and brothers. We speak blithely of the church as a family. But are we convinced that this is more than mere sentimentalism? Is the bond in Christ, which unites people of different races, languages, and nationalities, really more powerful than any other identification? The economic and political commitments of many Christians seem to belie such claims.

The eschatological vision of the Christian faith is that of a community in which all people are united in praise of Jesus Christ: "After this I looked, and there was a great multitude that no one could count, from every nation, from all tribes and peoples and languages, standing before the throne and before the Lamb, robed in white, with palm branches in their hands. They cried out in a loud voice, saying, 'Salvation belongs to our God who is seated on the throne, and to the Lamb!'" (Rv 7:9-10). The gospel of Jesus Christ propels its witnesses into all the world with the mission of uniting all people in this name. The failure of the church to fulfill this calling in no way negates the truth of the theological reality.

BEYOND NATIONALISM

The age of the Enlightenment brought into existence a revolutionary new form of human organization, the nation-state. In opposition to all forms of traditional authoritarianism, nations were to be ordered not by privileged classes who assume power according to wealth, property, or heredity, but by a contract between those governed and those who govern. By definition, a nation-state is a nation whose principle of organization is not language, tribe, or race but a contractual agreement among those who live there, that is, a state. Enlightenment thinkers sought to cast off Bible, pope, and king insofar as they restricted the free reign of human reason to structure human affairs.

Political theorists such as Thomas Hobbes and John Locke argued for government to be established according to mutual consent of the governed, with laws defined in constitutions limiting the power of those who rule. Nations were to be organized according to a reasoned agreement that defends the individual's rights to life, liberty, and property. The French and American revolutions gave birth to the models for all subsequent Western-style democracies. A nation came to be characterized by a constitution, bill of rights, participation of an electorate, legislature, judiciary, and executive branch.

Such an organization overcame many deficits of the ancient feudal system, securing rights for many who lacked them under previous systems of governance. For women and people of color, claiming these rights has meant a long and arduous struggle. Citizens governed under a system of law have avenues of recourse in changing current or advocating new legislation. They are to be afforded due process in defending themselves from accusations. Political and civil rights are protected by the authority of the state—for example, the freedoms of speech, assembly, or religion. The nation-state introduced a revolutionary new concept in contrast to traditional, hierarchical forms of political governance. The achievements of the democratic model in ordering human affairs, and especially in establishing checks and balances on the abuse of power, should not be undervalued.

In the realm of international affairs, however, the last two centuries have seen the steady emergence of the nation-state as the highest arbiter of worldly power. Even where adequate constitutional structures are lacking within a particular nation, the sovereignty of that nation-state in pursuing policies on behalf of its own self-interest has developed into an assumed dogma in international relationships. For the citizen of the nation-state, patriotism has come to entail unquestioning loyalty to the international policies of one's own nation insofar as these claim to involve national security.

In the United States, the identity of the nation-state has been powerfully shaped by an unofficial, though all-pervasive, civil religion. Civil religion in the United States is exercised through myths and rituals that provide a "sacred canopy" over all affairs of state (Peter Berger). The pledge of allegiance declares the United states as "one nation under God," and the nation's currency bears the imprint "in God we trust." National holidays, such as Independence Day and Memorial Day, are celebrated with many trappings of religious observance. Belief in God has become inextricably intertwined with loyalty to the nation.

The greatest dilemma posed to Christian faith by the nation-state and its civil religion is an idolatrous competition regarding what is ultimate. This is seen particularly in the arena of international relationships. The nation-state exacts a high price from those who resist its established policies, particularly (though not exclusively) in times of war. We need think only of the crisis of conscience faced by Dietrich Bonhoeffer during the church struggle in Nazi Germany. Bonhoeffer and the church in Germany faced the mutually exclusive choice: either loyalty to the nation or loyalty to Christ. Nations *always* operate with the conviction that their policies have divine authorization.

While a thorough treatment of the ethics of international affairs is beyond the scope of this chapter, we focus our attention on one particular aspect of international relations pertaining to those who share the Christian faith. This is not to say Christians are unconcerned about matters of universal human justice. More will be said about that in the chapter on social ministry. We refer here to the particular situation when one nation's policies have devastating consequences on people in another nation, especially on those who share the Christian faith. In this case there arises an acute dilemma for the Christian conscience. Does my ultimate loyalty rest with my nation and its claim to divine sanction or does my loyalty belong to my brothers and sisters in the one body of Christ, even though they are citizens of an enemy nation?

A strong theological argument can be made, based on the confession of faith in the catholicity of the church, that my greater loyalty is to those who share one common baptism. The consequences of such a conviction are manifold. The ultimacy of the state is relativized. National policies that endanger the well-being of brothers and sisters in Christ must be scrutinized and challenged. Civil disobedience is warranted where national hubris violates the safety of those "foreigners" who belong to the one body of Christ. Not only is the water of baptism thicker than the blood of kinship, but citizenship in the kingdom of God demands more sacred allegiance than that pledged to the flag.

The threat of idolatry that comes from the nation-state is one of the gravest challenges facing the contemporary church. To dissent from the identification of God and country is to commit an act of heresy. Yet loyalty to Jesus Christ means we take as seriously as did the early church that the discipleship of Jesus in the fellowship of the church takes precedence over our allegiance to Caesar. The most serious dilemmas facing the future of our earth—starvation, homelessness, disease, war, militarization, nuclear proliferation, environmental degradation—each remain unsolvable insofar as nation-states establish their own privileges as the highest good.

Christian people are needed to serve as leaven for thinking in terms larger than national self-interest and to do so for the theological reason that the church of Jesus Christ transcends all national boundaries. If we are to address the problems that summon our most urgent attention, we must increasingly recognize our global connectedness and do so beginning with the household of faith.

GLOBALIZATION AND THE CONGREGATION

To assert that the nation-state deserves only our penultimate allegiance is to teach an unconventional and subversive wisdom. Yet this is what a congregation affirms with every confession of the Nicene Creed. The history of the church and the story of the spread of the gospel instructs us in the global dimensions of Christian community. Christian congregations have the responsibility—and the ready opportunity—to broaden their vision and deepen their commitment to the catholicity of Christ's church.

The historic liturgy itself grounds one profoundly in the church catholic. To employ ancient words of Scripture from places named Sinai, Galilee, Jerusalem, and Patmos establishes connections with saints in distant locations. To pray traditional litanies, confess historic creeds, and chant ancient benedictions is to connect with all those throughout the world who over the centuries have joined in praising God with a single voice. To worship according to these liturgical forms is a powerful reminder of the catholicity of Christ's church. Not only do we connect ourselves with Christians in distant places from centuries past, but we express our unity with the whole catholic church throughout the world today, as they too participate in worshiping God through these forms.

There are numerous ways to accent the congregation's global connections through liturgical celebration. Intercessions can be offered on a regular basis for the needs of the church in other parts of the world—especially in concern for the needs of the hungry, in times of violent conflict, or in response to other moments of crisis. Another very direct way of establishing a global link is by the selection of music. Given a willingness to try new things, a congregation's worship can be enhanced by occasional use of musical settings of the liturgy originating from other cultures. Such ventures require thorough preparation. But there is great richness in discovering expressions of praise deriving from other tongues.

A less dramatic innovation is to introduce into the liturgy hymns and songs from the church in other parts of the world. These can be matched to the liturgical season and lectionary readings and introduced with reference to the significance of the song in its home country. The use of global music can be further enriched by the use of instrumentation appropriate to its original context. The images of God and Christ in such hymns and the images used to express the faith expand our own horizons in imagining ways we can more fully honor our God.

The use of artwork and the decor around the church building can contribute to global awareness. Pieces of art from churches in other parts of the world can be borrowed from those who own them or can be exchanged by mail. These can be displayed in a sanctuary or narthex and become a focal point for prayers offered on behalf of the church in that place. From time to time, new items can be introduced. Paraments and banners can also serve as vehicles for connecting with Christians in other parts of the world. A map of the world can be hung up in a prominent place and used to speak of missionary efforts or dilemmas faced by the church in other countries.

A congregation seeking to broaden its global connections can invite missionaries home from their assignments to come, teach, and preach about their experiences of the church in the places they have labored. Children and youth benefit greatly from this exposure to the global mission of the church. Where it is not already an annual congregational event, a "mission festival" can be organized, highlighting, at least for a Sunday or a week, the ministry of the church in a particular place, perhaps with a different focus every year. Seminaries or colleges may be able to provide lists of guest professors or international students who might be invited to make presentations as part of such a mission emphasis. Many local communities have representatives of other cultures already living in their midst who can be resources of information about the church in other parts of the world.

Representatives of congregations can also have their global awareness stretched by attending events held on a regional basis. Some denominations hold global mission events. Synodical gatherings frequently include greetings, sermons, and lectures by guests from partner churches. Those who attend such meetings can be given the opportunity to share with the entire congregation what they have learned about the challenges and accomplishments of the church's ministry in other contexts.

Members of the congregation who travel as tourists in other parts of the globe can be encouraged to make contact with Christians in the places where they visit in order to build up the vitality of the whole body of Christ. These relationships can become valuable sources of information about the needs of the church in other countries. Perhaps regular correspondence might even develop. One of the most amazing gifts of our catholic faith is the way relationships are freely developed with strangers from other races and nations as soon as one discovers that both share a common faith in Jesus Christ.

A more exacting involvement on the part of a congregation is to enter into mission support or mission partnership with a specific church in another part of the world. Denominations are ready resources for assisting congregations to identify projects worthy of their investment and can help establish contact. While the level of commitment required of mission partners is greater than with the other ideas already mentioned, the level of satisfaction is greater as well. The ongoing contact with a partner church and the relationships that develop among Christians who share each others' faith is an incomparable blessing. Often such partnerships eventually lead to visits by representatives of the respective communities.

These are but some of the ways a local congregation might explore its global connections within the one catholic church. A global vision helps bring our practice into conformity with our confession of faith in the catholicity of Christ's church. Moreover, our own faith and ministry are enhanced by the gifts Christians in other parts of the world have to offer to us. For one, as we discover how the Christian gospel is being contextualized in other cultures, we learn how we can better contextualize mission in our own particular setting.

Not least of all, Christians in other parts of the world need our prayers, encouragement, and material support. The disparity of material blessings among the peoples and nations across the globe remains one of the greatest scandals of the modern world. Christians, related by baptism with brothers and sisters on other continents, can be advocates for a humane foreign policy on the part of government. By virtue of this relatedness to people in other parts of the world, the church of Jesus Christ can be a voice for diplomacy and peaceful resolution of conflict in a world where nations too readily resort to violence in attempting to settle their differences. While the scale of a congregation's involvement in making global connections must be matched to local circumstances, every congregation can be enriched by developing the global dimension of the church's confession of faith.

FOR FURTHER READING

Balasuriya, Tissa. *Planetary Theology.* Maryknoll: Orbis, 1984.

Bosch, David J. *Transforming Mission: Paradigm Shifts in Theology of Mission.* Maryknoll, Orbis, 1991.

Brown, Robert McAfee, ed. *Kairos: Three Prophetic Challenges to the Church.* Grand Rapids: Eerdmans, 1990.

Donovan, Vincent J. *The Church in the Midst of Creation.* Maryknoll: Orbis, 1989.

Evans, Alice Frazer; Evans, Robert A.; and Kennedy, William Bean. *Pedagogies for the Non-Poor.* Maryknoll: Orbis, 1990.

Ferm, Deane William. *Third World Liberation Theologies: An Introductory Survey.* Maryknoll: Orbis, 1986.

Galdamez, Pablo. *Faith of a People: The Life of a Basic Christian Community in El Salvador.* Maryknoll: Orbis, 1986.

Neal, Marie Augusta. *The Just Demands of the Poor: Essays in Socio-Theology.* New York: Paulist, 1987.

Nessan, Craig L. *Orthopraxis or Heresy: The North American Theological Response to Latin American Liberation Theology.* Atlanta: Scholars, 1989.

Sanneh, Lamin. *Translating the Message: The Missionary Impact on Culture.* Maryknoll: Orbis, 1989.

TEN

ECUMENISM: THAT ALL MAY BE ONE

The great watchword of the ecumenical movement in the twentieth century is uttered by Jesus as a petition of his high-priestly prayer in John 17:20-21: "I ask not only on behalf of these, but also on behalf of those who will believe in me through their word, *that they may all be one.* As you, Father, are in me and I am in you, may they also be in us, so that the world may believe that you have sent me." Notice in this prayer that the unity of the church is not formulated as an end in itself. Rather, Jesus prays for the unity of the church for the sake of mission. The unity of the persons in the Holy Trinity serves as an analogy for understanding the unity of the church with God. And the church's unity in God serves as powerful testimony for the sake of the world, "that the world may believe" in Jesus as the one God has sent.

Christ entrusted to the church the sacraments of Baptism and Eucharist as signs of its oneness with him. All who have been baptized in the name of Christ have been baptized into one body and made to drink of one Spirit (1 Cor 12:13). Likewise Paul queries the congregation in Corinth: "The cup of blessing that we bless, is it not a sharing in the blood of Christ? The bread that we break, is it not a sharing in the body of Christ? Because there is one bread, we who are many are one body, for we all partake of the one bread" (1 Cor 10:16-17).

Yet one does not need to know much about the Christian church (such as the one at Corinth) to learn that these very sacraments of unity have been the source of bitter argument and deep division throughout its history. The splintering of the church into thousands of denominations, sects, and factions acts as one of the greatest obstacles to belief on the part of the world. The church's fragmentation makes a mockery of Jesus' prayer and of the sacraments he instituted.

If the world is to believe that Jesus is indeed the one sent by God, the ecumenical task remains an urgent priority. Ever more, the responsibility for ecumenical rapprochement shifts from official dialogues and interconfessional agreements to the local level where the implications of reconciliation have immediate and concrete ramifications. How can we continue to confess our faith in the words of the Nicene Creed—"We believe in the one . . . church"—and continue to exist in alienation and even antagonism with other members of the one body of Christ?

ECUMENISM AS APOLOGETICS

"Why should I believe all this stuff when you Christians can't even get along with each other?" In these or similar words, the divisions within the church give offense (and excuse!) to non-believers. Whether it be Protestants and Roman Catholics in Northern Ireland, unreconciled Lutheran church bodies in the United States, or the proselytizing of the "non-denominational" church down the street, the fragmentation of the church is a scandal to skeptics—as it ought to be to Christians themselves.

One should not confuse this proposal about the unity of the church with an attempt to impose uniformity. Already preceding the formation of the New Testament canon, the church had attained a rich diversity of communal expressions, reflected in the variety of theological images used to interpret God's reality as revealed in the person and work of Jesus. Moreover, local communities of faith accented different aspects of the Christian tradition according to the unique circumstances and the diverse problems confronting them. Thus each of the four Gospel writers—Matthew, Mark, Luke, and John—formulated their version of the Jesus story in correlation with the issues facing the particular community familiar to them. In a parallel way, Paul writes letters with varying theological images and specific practical instruction depending on the situation in the congregation he is addressing.

A strong argument can be made that the major confessional differences among the various churches can be explained on the basis of the New Testament itself. The variety of outlooks and theological positions within the canon itself accounts for a large portion of the significant divergences of belief among the major denominations. Thus Lutherans focus on the Pauline doctrine of justification by grace through faith, Presbyterians on glorifying God in worship and life, Methodists on living a sanctified life, and Pentecostals on the extraordinary gifts of the Holy Spirit. Each of these emphases (as well as others) has a legitimate place among the varied writings in the New Testament canon. Different "canons within the canon" lead various church bodies in distinct theological directions. Taken to their logical conclusions, these contrasting points of orientation serve to explain many of the confessional differences among the Christian denominations.

A reconciled church would need to make provision for a similar range of theological interpretations, varieties of piety, and differences of church order as evidenced in the New Testament itself. Yet within such a church there would also exist a mutual affirmation of the legitimacy of one another's ministries that is sorely lacking between so many churches in the present. The greatest affront of all is the failure on the part of churches to recognize one another's baptism. To rebaptize someone from another tradition is tantamount to denying that other tradition is Christian.

A similar argument can be made with regard to the failure of Christians to welcome one another to their celebrations of the Lord's supper. One would do well to ask whether a celebration of the Lord's supper at which some of the baptized (that is, those from another denomination) are not welcome is a legitimate celebration at all. The Jesus who ate at table with tax collectors and sinners scandalized only the Pharisees. The Jesus who shared a meal with his disciples the night before his death was crucified for all. Jesus' supper is to be a meal for the forgiveness of sin and the reconciliation of the estranged. How tragic that we have invented reasons for turning it into an occasion for excluding members of Christ's body who happen to belong to another denomination!

Although the first great schism of the church occurred in 1054 with the division between the Orthodox and Roman Catholic churches, it is the fallout from the Protestant Reformation that led to the bewildering array of sects and brands of churches with which we are today confronted. While the return to the central doctrine of justification by grace through faith was an absolutely necessary correction insisted upon by the reformers within the late-medieval church, the consequences for the unity of the church have been disastrous. To introduce the principle of conscience as the sole basis for determining the legitimacy of a particular interpretation of Scripture opened the floodgates to a torrent of waters wreaking destruction upon the church's oneness. Each and every religious visionary can claim a special revelation of divine truth and proclaim it with such intensity that some are persuaded into following.

The churches of the Reformation, and particularly the Lutherans among them, bear a special measure of responsibility for the frag-

menting of the church in subsequent centuries. This in no way is to
negate the historical necessity of the reforms demanded by Luther of
the Roman Catholic Church in the sixteenth century. It is rather to
honestly confess the Protestant share of responsibility for the loss of
church unity, which was an unforeseeable yet tragic consequence of
the Reformation heritage. For this reason Protestants—and particularly Lutherans—have a special obligation to commit themselves to
the reconciliation of Christ's church. By God's grace, Lutherans may
also be uniquely situated to serve as a bridge in the process of reconciliation between those churches with the "historic episcopate" and
other Reformed churches who share Lutheran commitment to the
authority of Scripture alone.

For the sake of the gospel and Christian mission in the twenty-first
century—a century likely to see yet further erosion of Christian influence—ecumenism emerges as an apologetic task of the first order. What
is more, only a reconciled Christian church, in which the mission of Jesus
Christ is put ahead of denominational wrangling, will be adequately prepared for the societal and environmental problems of this new century.

TOWARD A COMMON TABLE

As one surveys the alienation among church bodies during the first
four hundred years following the Reformation, the progress toward
reuniting divided Christendom accomplished in the last fifty years is
remarkable. When at Amsterdam in 1948 two monumental ecumenical
movements, "Faith and Order" and "Life and Work," united in the formation of the World Council of Churches (WCC), this marked the cul-
mination of a process that had been fermenting for decades, even prior to
the war. Following a pattern of holding global assemblies approxi-
mately every seven years, the WCC defined itself with these words at
New Delhi in 1961: "The World Council of Churches is a fellowship of
churches which confess the Lord Jesus Christ as God the Savior according to the Scriptures and therefore seek to fulfill together their common
calling to the glory of the one God, Father, Son and Holy Spirit."

The scope of the WCC expanded greatly beginning in 1960 when
Pope John XXIII authorized the involvement of the Roman Catholic
Church in the ecumenical movement by forming the Society for Promoting Christian Unity. Further sanction was offered to Roman Catholic
involvement by the Decree on Ecumenism, adopted at the Second Vatican

Council in 1964. Now the deliberations of the WCC could include not only Protestant and Orthodox but also Roman Catholic representation.

One of the fruits of the ecumenical movement has been the promotion and organization of bilateral and multilateral dialogues among church bodies. The purpose of such conversations has been to search for what convictions churches share in common, while not minimizing those issues that continue to divide. The results of these dialogues have been published in numerous volumes, many of which have been given official status by church bodies.

Perhaps the most important of all of these products of ecumenical discussion has been the convergence proposal, *Baptism, Eucharist and Ministry,* disseminated to the churches as a result of an action by the Commission on Faith and Order of the WCC meeting at Lima in 1982. This document called for all churches to respond to its formulation of a proposed consensus position regarding the key issues of baptism, Eucharist, and ministry. The question posed was a crucial one: "To what extent can your church recognize in this text the faith of the Church through the ages?" It is exactly this sort of exacting question that can move the churches to self-examination regarding the fullness of their own positions and acknowledge the legitimacy of Christian truth in other bodies. Again this proposal evoked a voluminous literature of responses.

Efforts of the WCC like this one, together with the many bilateral and multilateral dialogues, have borne exceptional fruit in increasing mutual understanding and cooperation among the divided churches. Specific proposals continue to come before denominational assemblies seeking ratification. The central problem with this process has been, however, the failure of the reception process to proceed from the denominational to the local level. The true test for the success of the ecumenical movement is now located on the level of relationships among local congregations in local communities throughout the world. Insofar as the groundwork for ecumenical rapprochement has not been carefully developed on the local level, the adoption of new and innovative proposals—especially those that have substantive impact on local communities—will be difficult.

The future of the ecumenical movement shifts increasingly to local congregations, who must assume responsibility for deliberating what unity means among the churches in a particular place. Guided by the careful statements of theologians and church executives, congregations need to encourage substantive conversation in their local communities to discover the implications of ecumenical dialogue for their own specific congregations. Already this has taken place to a certain degree in many places. But the initiatives have often been cursory rather than involving our best efforts at preparation and study. Where significant discussion has evolved, congregational leaders need to communicate the results to denominational representatives.

One perennial danger of the congregation is parochialism. We become so preoccupied with our own inner life as a congregation that it is difficult to generate the energy needed to initiate programs between congregations, particularly with those of another denomination. Perhaps the only cure for such lethargy is to immerse ourselves ever deeper in Jesus' high priestly prayer, so that our hearts be converted to the urgency of the ecumenical task for the sake of Christian mission.

A glance in any local phone directory will amaze the reader at the wide array of churches listed in the yellow pages. In most vicinities an interdenominational ministerium likely exists. These provide one forum for ecumenical discussion, although the wide range of viewpoints at such gatherings may make substantive discussion laborious. Such organizations are often much more adept at cooperating on practical efforts at Christian charity than entering into serious theological discussion. If we probe too deeply we might soon discover how greatly our interpretations of the faith separate us! This is not to dismiss efforts to promote theologically motivated ecumenical discussion among ministerial alliances. It is only to acknowledge the difficulty of the enterprise.

A more manageable approach to local ecumenical efforts begins with a limited number of congregations, perhaps only two. Insofar as these come from traditions that have engaged in dialogue on the denominational level, the published resources from such discussions are invaluable for deepening the conversation. Those who give leadership to whatever meetings are planned among the churches must give careful attention to such materials. One aim of local ecumenical conversation is to measure the degree to which the issues that occupy formal denominational discussion do indeed inform the differences that exist in local practice. Sometimes one discovers that on the local level what unites and what divides are based on factors quite different from what one would assume based on confessional traditions.

One valuable result of local ecumenical conversations are the human relationships that develop out of such encounters. Something that inhibits enthusiasm for ecumenical events among congregations is the fear by members of demonstrating ignorance about one's own tradition or disclosing the vices of one's congregation in the presence of another. The contrary, however, is virtually always the result. We discover in conversation with others how much we already implicitly know about our own traditions and, moreover, how committed we are to the congregation to which we belong. The relationships we establish with Christians from a congregation in another tradition only enhance our own experience of community in Christ.

Relationships between congregations must be nurtured over a long period of time. While not wanting to spread one's efforts too thin, a congregation may be able to pursue the development of more than one ecumenical relationship at a time, working separately with congregations that come from distinct traditions. Careful attention needs to be paid to the agendas for the time spent together. The meetings must not be allowed to degenerate into mere socializing but rather focus on issues that lead to deeper understanding of one another's traditions and to ventures in inter-congregational cooperation.

One central goal of ecumenical relationships between local congregations is the planning and holding of joint worship services. These should be scheduled at a time that encourages maximum participation from congregation members. That means considering Sunday morning as a prime time to hold common worship. What better witness to the community at large about the unity of Christ's church than to organize and publicize shared worship on a Sunday morning!

Certainly other times also offer advantages. The festivals of Epiphany and Ascension are often under-observed by congregations, and excitement for worship on these days can be stimulated by planning a joint service. Reformation Day (or Sunday) can offer an occasion for congregations from different reformation traditions to celebrate their heritage. All Saints Day provides an occasion for churches of every denomination to emphasize their unity and may be a particularly good time for Roman Catholics to join with Protestants at worship. Pentecost affords the opportunity to accent the gifts poured upon the church by the Holy Spirit, including the gift of unity. Congregations that do not observe the liturgical year have their own patterns, which may give reason to an ecumenical observance at a given time of year. Good Friday has become an occasion for community-wide services. Of course, national holidays, such as Thanksgiving, may give impetus to ecumenical services that otherwise would not take place.

Prior to such ecumenical worship, careful planning must take place to ensure that those involved will understand and appreciate the ritual action. For example, what one tradition assumes to belong to the standard repertoire of hymnody may prove to be totally unfamiliar to those from another tradition. Unspoken assumptions can be extremely dangerous. The congregation hosting an ecumenical service should probably take the lead in ordering the worship to be held in its own worship space, using a liturgy from its own tradition. At the same time, every effort should be spent to inform members of the other congregation(s) about the ritual practices and their meaning. Members of the guest congregation(s) can be invited to lead portions of the service where appropriate. The clergy of both congregations can share the leadership in a way that demonstrates mutual affirmation of one another's ministries. On another occasion, the roles between host and guest congregations can be reversed.

The ultimate expression of congregational unity in Christ occurs around the Lord's table. Where denominations have reached agreements regarding table fellowship, a common celebration of the Eucharist provides the culminating symbol of Christian unity. Thankfully, a number of Christian traditions have reached the point where their communion tables are officially open to members of other denominations, at least to certain ones. Again, such mutual celebrations of the Lord's supper must be carefully planned by the participating churches, lest differences in practice undermine the unity contained in the symbols of one loaf and one cup.

Where denominational differences do not yet permit eucharistic sharing (or even common worship), may our hunger for sharing this universal Christian meal motivate us to renewed efforts at reconciliation! What a tragedy if the first time we come together at table will be in God's heaven!

IN SERVICE TO GOD'S WORLD

Concerted efforts at community service are a powerful form of Christian witness by congregations of varied denominations. We recall Jesus' prayer that the church be one in order that the world might believe that Jesus is the one sent from God. Common acts of

Christian charity by congregations in a local community thus have a twofold purpose. First, the purpose is to be responsive to pressing human need in that community. Those who are hungry, homeless, lacking clothing, discriminated against, addicted, or abused need both the material help and advocacy efforts that Christian churches can provide. Second, however, this ministry to human need is itself a form of witness to the power of Christ alive in that place.

Churches should neither use their evangelistic motive to manipulate those to whom they minister, nor remain silent about the name of the one they seek to serve. To balance genuine concern for those in physical need with a holistic concern also for the soul requires tremendous integrity of purpose. Cooperative efforts on the part of churches often are threatened by disagreements about the way acts of mercy should serve the cause of evangelism. On the one extreme are those who make material help conditional upon listening to an evangelistic message. On the other extreme are those who avoid naming the name of Jesus altogether. Finding a middle ground between these extremes, cooperative efforts at Christian charity do and ought to make clear witness to Jesus as the one sent by God. Clarity from the outset about how charity and evangelism are to be related will help avoid tension in an ecumenical venture at social outreach.

The specific needs of a particular community should set the agenda for which projects a local ecumenical organization ought to undertake. In virtually every community, there exists a pressing need to respond to the hungry, the homeless, those discriminated against, the abused, the addicted, and the transient. Given the cutbacks in government services, the urgency of a response by Christians has increased in recent years. The weight of human need may appear to far surpass the resources of the church to respond. For this reason, it is wise for leaders of ecumenical efforts to analyze carefully which needs are most pressing and which needs the group is best equipped to meet given the resources available.

One value of cooperative effort when responding to the hungry, homeless, and transient is the ability to ensure good stewardship of resources. A coordinated effort helps avoid duplication of services among individual congregations. Common record keeping can assist in tracking the assistance given to various individuals and families in order to balance the distribution of limited resources. Those eligible for government services can be more easily identified and referred. Not least of all, those who contribute their resources to the support of local charity gain confidence that a more effective use is being made of their gifts.

Local ecumenical efforts need not always start from scratch in developing programs of social outreach. Church World Service can assist in coordinating local efforts on behalf of the hungry through its CROP Walk program. This program, which can become an annual event, both raises awareness of the needs of the hungry and provides an effective way of raising funds. Habitat for Humanity is another nationwide organization that can give direction to local efforts, in this case in response to the homeless. Apart from such large-scale organizations, the models of social ministry developed in other nearby communities can help give direction to local initiatives.

Community-wide efforts to develop food pantries, homeless shelters, safe houses for abused women and children, treatment centers for the addicted, or assistance for transients are not the only possible results of ecumenical cooperation among local congregations. Where as few as two congregations are willing to work together, perhaps as a result of a carefully nurtured partnership, valuable fruits can become manifest. Examples of projects that can be undertaken by as few as two congregations include a shared program of Christian education (for example, Vacation Bible School), the formation of a pre-school, cooperation in making quilts for use in local shelters or overseas, outreach among youth, or a soup kitchen for the hungry.

Given the incredible cost of building and maintaining a facility, one of the most wise stewardship decisions that two congregations might make would be to choose to share the use of a single building. Such a decision requires a congregation to be clear that its identity is not grounded in its exclusive use of a particular building. Instead it challenges a congregation to think anew about what it means for the members themselves to be the body of Christ with Jesus as the head. Where two congregations come to the point where they so fully affirm one another's ministries that such foundational sharing is possible, again a powerful witness is made to a local community.

Another dimension of ecumenical witness involves public advocacy on behalf of the marginalized and oppressed in a given community. With regard to most controversial issues advocating social change, it will prove difficult for a ministerial association to come to a consensus on a given course of action. Instead, certain members of congregations may well come together to work for advocacy according to their particular vision of a better future. Further comment on the place of ecumenical efforts in the advocacy of public policy will be reserved for the final chapter.

The theology of the congregation here proposed elevates the role of ecumenism to a status seldom attained by congregations in the present. Ecumenism becomes one of the key expressions of a congregation's mission. In part, this is due to the exigencies of mission in the emerging post-Christian era. But even more fundamentally it is in response to the intention of Jesus that the church be one. The scandal of a divided Christendom cannot serve the mission of the one Lord, Jesus Christ. We are called to rediscover the oneness of baptism as we gather around a common Lord's table, in order to witness to Jesus as the one sent by God for the salvation of the entire world. United in this mission we stand; divided we fall.

FOR FURTHER READING

Anderson, H. George, and Crumley, James R., Jr., eds. *Promoting Unity: Themes in Lutheran-Catholic Dialogue.* Minneapolis: Augsburg, 1989.

Bilheimer, Robert S. *Breakthrough: The Emergence of the Ecumenical Tradition.* Grand Rapids: Eerdmans, 1989.

Bluck, John. *Everyday Ecumenism: Can You Take the World Church Home?* Geneva: WCC Publications, 1987.

Burgess, Joseph A., ed. *In Search of Christian Unity: Basic Consensus/Basic Differences.* Minneapolis: Fortress, 1991.

Kinnamon, Michael, ed. *Signs of the Spirit: World Council of Churches Official Report – Seventh Assembly.* Geneva: WCC Publications, 1991.

Lazareth, William H. *Baptism, Eucharist and Ministry.* Faith and Order Paper No. 111. Geneva: WCC Publications, 1982.

Lehmann, Karl, and Pannenberg, Wolfhart. *The Condemnations of the Reformation Era: Do They Still Divide?* Minneapolis: Fortress, 1990.

Meyer, Harding, and Vischer, Lukas, eds. *Growth in Agreement: Reports and Agreed Statements of Ecumenical Conversations on a World Level.* New York: Paulist, 1984.

Raiser, Konrad. *Ecumenism in Transition: A Paradigm Shift in the Ecumenical Movement?* Geneva: WCC Publications, 1991.

Rusch, William G. *Ecumenism: A Movement Toward Church Unity.* Philadelphia: Fortress, 1985.

ELEVEN

SOCIAL MINISTRY: STRIVING FOR JUSTICE AND PEACE IN ALL THE EARTH

"Do you intend to continue in the covenant God made with you in Holy Baptism: to live among God's faithful people...and to strive for justice and peace in all the earth?"

So one promises according to the rite of the Affirmation of Baptism, used at services of baptismal renewal by all the baptized, for the reception of new members, and especially for confirmation. To make such a promise is a tall order for one mature in the Christian faith, let alone a fourteen-year-old on confirmation day. This question aims to promote nothing less than the public responsibility of Christians in the world.

Yet to enter into the sphere of public policy is to tread among serpents. The conviction remains strong among the baptized that a strict distinction must be maintained between church and state. This provision, which was intended to prevent the establishment of a state religion in the United States, is taken to preclude the church from taking a stand on social issues. To advocate that the church as a whole, or even that an individual congregation, take a position with regard to a controversial public issue is to invite snakebite. Leaders of congregations who seek to fulfill the charge to strive for justice and peace in all the earth enter an arena that is highly contested and politically polarized. While the ministry of a congregation is impoverished by the failure to enter the fray, those who give leadership in such matters are called upon to follow the injunction of Jesus to "be wise as serpents and innocent as doves" (Mt 10:16).

Jesus leaves no room for the weak-hearted, however, when it comes to the task of social ministry. In one of the most frequently cited texts of liberation theology, we are summoned to the very judgment seat of Christ (Mt 25:31-45). Christ sits upon the throne of glory and separates the sheep from the goats, the saved from the damned. On what basis does Christ render judgment? On the basis of whether the members of the church rendered him service in this world. And how did they render Christ service? On the basis of whether the hungry neighbor was fed, the thirst of the neighbor was quenched, the stranger was welcomed, the naked were clothed, the sick received ministry, and the prisoner was visited. For, you see, "as you did it to one of the least of these who are members of my family, you did it to me" (Mt 25:40). While the sheep in the parable were surprised to discover that Christ appeared in the form of the "least of these," we have an advantage they did not have and are therefore without excuse. We have the witness of the one who has risen from the dead (cf. Lk 16:31), who instructs us with this imperative of neighbor love.

SOCIAL SERVICE AND SOCIAL ADVOCACY

When speaking of congregational social ministry, a fundamental distinction needs to be made between two expressions: social service and social advocacy. By "social service" we refer to those forms of social ministry that provide direct assistance to relieve human need. One might think immediately of disaster relief, hunger programs, medical assistance, or housing projects. Also falling into this category are many of the common functions of denominational social service agencies: adoption programs, counseling services, refugee resettlement, job training, homeless shelters, sheltered workshops for people with disabilities, assistance to people who are blind or deaf, support for single parents, programs for the elderly, and a host of other charitable works.

Congregations participate in an essential way in social service through their financial support and volunteer efforts given to denominational, regional, and ecumenical programs organized to offer direct relief to the various kinds of human suffering and need. A local congregation might also have within its own purview such ministries as a food pantry, day care center, parochial school or pre-school, short-term housing shelter, refugee sponsorship, safe house, or providing funds for those in acute need (for example, travelers' aid, utilities assistance, rent assistance, and so forth). This is to leave unmentioned the ministry provided by members of a congregation, one for another, that lends emotional, material, and spiritual support in times of crisis (at the time of illness, death, accident, disaster, job loss, marital crisis, depression, and so on). A "ministry of presence" to those who suffer acute human need can itself be a vital form of congregational social ministry.

All of these varieties of "social service" are essential, necessary, and exemplary demonstrations of social ministry. Congregational support for such programs on a local, regional, and global level provides a powerful witness about Christian compassion to those in need. Through these efforts great human suffering finds relief. Such activities, moreover, provide an outlet for Christian charity that builds upon strong precedents from the history of the church. A clear consensus for these kinds of programs tends to emerge naturally within the life of a congregation.

When we turn to social advocacy, however, we enter an arena that is highly contested. By "social advocacy" we mean efforts on the part of the church to change societal structures, promote economic policies, or enact legislation that is consistent with its understanding of the kingdom of God. The charters of organizations like Bread for the World and Amnesty International provide a reference point for this distinctive type of social ministry. Denominational advocacy efforts with regard to racism, sexism, heterosexism, poverty, hunger, homelessness, violence, war, arms proliferation, prisons, capital punishment, environmental concerns, and so forth fall into this category. Likewise congregations, or members thereof, may wish to raise their voices on behalf of a particular cause that entails changing societal structures.

Unlike proposals involving social service efforts, however, congregations often have a difficult time coming to a consensus around questions of social advocacy. The provision for the separation of church and state in the U.S. Constitution is often interpreted to deny church advocacy with regard to political, economic, and social themes. While this is a misinterpretation of the disestablishment clause (its purpose being to forbid the state from establishing a favored religion), confusion about or resistance to congregational advocacy efforts is common on the part of many members.

This situation of misunderstanding the church's efforts in social advocacy requires a critical reappraisal. The biblical tradition bears witness to an extraordinary "justice trajectory" that warrants the church's involvement in advocacy on behalf of the poor, the victim, the marginalized, and the oppressed. Beginning with the exodus narrative, God hears and responds to the groaning of Hebrew slaves (Ex 2:23-25) and acts to set them free from Pharaoh's oppression (Ex 3:7-9). A notable feature of the law by which Israel was to live out its covenant relationship with this God is the provision by which there is to be special protection for the widow, orphan, and "resident alien" (Ex 22:21-24). The poor likewise receive protection from paying exploitative interest and from excessive demands for "security deposits" on loans (Ex 22:25-27). Two of the most exceptional aspects of the Levitical code are the standards for a sabbatical year and a year of jubilee (Lev 25). Both of these provisions are based on the conviction that God ultimately owns all. Accordingly, in the seventh year the land is to lie fallow, and the economy is to be sustained only by what has been stored and by the fields' natural yield (25:1-7). More extraordinary still is the account of the "jubilee year," to be observed every fiftieth year, in which all debts were to be canceled and property returned to ancestral estates (25:8-24).

When Israel came to the conclusion that it would be organized around the rule of a king—a decision about which controversy prevailed for fear of the king's abuse of power—it was done with the expectation that the king would himself serve God's law with its demand for justice (2 Sm 8:15; 1 Kgs 10:9). Several of the psalms hold up the expectation that the king advocate justice and righteousness, especially in defense of the poor and oppressed (Pss 58, 72, 82). At the very same time as Israel adopted the monarchy, there emerged simultaneously the office of prophet as a check on the potential abuses of royal power. The oracles of the prophets redound with the demand that Israel and its ruler do justice (for example, Mi 3:9-12; Jer 22:13-16; Is 42:5-7). The Messiah for whom Israel longed was to be an executor of justice and peace (Is 11:1-9).

This strong justice trajectory within the Hebrew Bible finds its continuation in the ministry of Messiah Jesus. In Luke's gospel, for example, Jesus is programmatically identified as the fulfillment of Isaiah's messianic expectations in his inaugural sermon at Nazareth (Lk 4:16-21). Jesus' teachings contain a powerful message of justice for the poor and judgment upon the rich (Lk 6:20-26; 12:15-21, 33-34; 16:13, 19-31; 18:22-25; 19:1-10). Jesus provokes his opponents by driving the sellers out of the temple, declaring: "My house shall be a house of prayer; but you have made it a den of robbers" (Lk 19:45-46). Jesus is renowned as the friend of tax collectors and sinners who eat with him at table (Lk 15:1-2). In accordance with covenantal law, Jesus advocates the cause of the poor, the sick, the marginalized, the oppressed. Luke witnesses that in Jesus' ministry the messianic age has arrived.

While this justice trajectory is upheld in the synoptic traditions and to a certain degree in the other traditions of the earliest church (Acts 2:42-47; 4:32-37), the New Testament expectation of an imminent parousia raised a challenge to every attempt at justifying ministry aimed at social transformation (1 Thes 4:13-18). The expectation of the return of Jesus as the Son of Man to bring history to its conclusion undercut efforts at working for social change (1 Cor 7:17-24). Why invest in the structures of an age that is soon to pass away? Charity offered in relief of human suffering is always salutary. But to advocate the change of social structures within the context of Roman oppression, especially within a scenario of imminent apocalyptic destruction and deliverance, was unfathomable (Rv 22:12-21).

Contrary to the expectations of first-century Christians, we have seen the unfolding of two thousand years of Christian history. While some will continue to insist that the return of Christ is yet imminent (all the more under the specter of a new millennium), can we continue to allow the eschatological expectations of the first century to deter the church from investing its serious efforts in transforming the structures of this world on behalf of justice? This is not to argue for any utopian scheme by which Christians can themselves construct the kingdom of God. Rather, it is to argue that the church rightfully has a warrant to engage in social advocacy according to the justice trajectory inherited from Israel and sustained in the ministry of Jesus. While the most we can ever hope for in this world are approximations of God's justice, many lives are salvaged by reasoned efforts to establish more just social structures.

In anticipation of the continuation of history, we take our bearings for social advocacy not from New Testament apocalyptic but from the Hebrew notion of *shalom*. The word *shalom* expresses that the divine purpose for this world is that all created beings live together in justice, righteousness, and peace. The salvation that God intends is not an escape from this world but rather its transformation. *Shalom* entails a holistic understanding of salvation in which body and spirit, the individual and society, the human and nonhuman, the religious and the political are all incorporated. God seeks to work "total well-being" for the entire creation (Folk).

THE CRITICAL MASS: THREE PRIORITIES

Taking cues from the Eucharist liturgy and the contemporary context, we propose three priorities for congregational social ministry. The structure of the Eucharist—as we in worship "pretend" the kingdom of God—provides a mirror in which we see the conditions of our world more clearly. The "mass" thus contains a "critical" element; it helps us see our world in the light of God's *shalom*. The three features of the liturgy to which we attend are: (1) the offering of the created gifts of bread and wine for the meal, (2) the sharing of the food around the table, and (3) the passing of the peace of Christ within the community and beyond.

First, the offering of elements from God's good creation for the meal symbolizes the responsibility of Christians to care for God's world. One offertory prayer reminds the worshiping community to be dedicated to the care of all God has made. In recent years there have been poignant reminders that there are limits to the earth's ability to recover from abuse. Natural resources can be depleted. Plant and animal species do become extinct. Pollution does damage not only the quality of the air we breathe but even the ozone layer. Water can be made hazardous for creaturely consumption and habitation. Nuclear materials pose a long-term threat to life in all its manifestations. All of life co-exists in delicate symbiotic relationships. When one part of the ecosystem suffers, all members of the system suffer together (cf. 1 Cor 12).

Congregations have a responsibility to God to care for the portion of God's creation entrusted into their stewardship. This begins with care for the congregation's own property and grounds but extends far beyond. Congregations can do much to educate proper care for the earth, sky, and sea. Members can hear, for example, about recycling efforts and the responsible reduction and disposal of waste. They can take seriously the environmental impact of congregational decisions. They can take the perspective of a steward of God's creation into their homes and their places of employment.

More than local efforts, however, congregations can encourage members to become advocates for legislation consistent with sound stewardship of God's world. There exist a number of groups that alert a broad membership regarding the environmental implications of public decisions. Suggestions are offered for intelligent advocacy on behalf of the creation upon which we all depend for life. Congregations can themselves become vehicles for communicating matters of public policy to members.

Second, the sharing of bread and wine around the communion table serves as a powerful reminder of the responsibility to feed hungry neighbors. We live in a hungry world. Jesus fed the multitudes (Mk 6:30-44; 8:1-10). Can we begin to assimilate what it means that 40,000 hungry neighbors continue to die every day from hunger and its related causes? Over one billion human beings are seriously malnourished in our world. The scale of human hunger exceeds our capacity to fathom. Hunger is a scandal that has lost its ability to shock our consciences. All current statistics, moreover, indicate the disparity between the rich and poor, the "haves" and "have nots," is only increasing. Population numbers rise while the willingness of the privileged to share declines. Violence against the earth—pollution, soil erosion, desertification, resource depletion—together with the use of inappropriate technology reduces the amount of food that agriculture can produce. Feedlot cattle eat grain while human beings starve. Will the amount of suffering related to hunger be so magnified in coming decades that the church will be compelled to declare response to the hungry a matter of *status confessionis*?

Congregations are obligated to include ministry to hungry neighbors at the heart of their social ministry. This begins with relief to hungry members of the congregation itself. Resources can be made available to assist in the feeding of needy individuals and families. Local food pantries provide a way to extend this concern into the larger community. Many congregations may also choose to participate in meal delivery programs (for example, "Meals-on-Wheels"). These and other forms of direct relief to hungry people belong to the identity and mission of those who seek to serve in the name of the one who fed the crowds.

If the dimensions of the hunger dilemma are to begin to be addressed, however, members of congregations will need to become increasingly committed to involvement in hunger issues on a larger scale. Support for denominational hunger programs at a significant level of financial commitment is fundamental. Such programs address systemic issues, which need to be taken into account in any effective stewardship of resources. Denominational programs aim both at direct relief of hunger and at the development of local economies so that people become capacitated to feed themselves.

Furthermore, members of congregations need to become educated on the impact legislation has on the hungry, both domestically and globally. Just as Jesus expressed particular concern for the poor in his ministry, so the church of Jesus has the responsibility to act as advocate for the poor who have lost the voice to speak for themselves. Citizens have become woefully inept at examining legislation according to any other criterion than self-interest. As Robert Bellah and others have argued, we desperately need to recover a notion of the common good. Members of congregations need to learn to measure and evaluate all legislation according to its impact on the poor of this world. Such advocacy is a matter not only of Christian charity but of self-interest in order to secure stable political and economic structures.

Third, the liturgical passing of the peace within the Eucharist service symbolizes the imperative that Christians act as peacemakers (Mt 5:9). Not only are we to be at peace with one another before we come to the table, but, as we meet in the supper the one who is the Prince of Peace, we are filled with a peace that makes us advocates of peace.

Violence permeates every level of society. Domestic violence invades the home. The media portray countless acts of violence that make it appear commonplace. Neighborhoods are stalked by gang violence. Weapons proliferate in our homes, work places, and even schools. Violent crime seems rampant and random. Society retaliates against violent crime by capital punishment. Terrorist acts maim and kill the innocent. New forms of tribalism threaten to further disintegrate the social fabric, turning each faction against all others. War, buttressed by weapons with unimaginable destructive force, continues to break out season after season. Each new war is always declared a righteous cause, with the name of God regularly invoked as rationale for each nation's involvement.

Of all peoples, Christians are those who ought to see through the rationalizations used to justify acts of violence. At the core of Christian conviction lies the cross of Jesus, which testifies to the violent death of an innocent man. Recent scholarship, under inspiration from the work of René Girard, has unmasked the proclivity of human beings to resolve tension and rivalry within society by acts of "sacred violence." As the ancient Jewish ritual of scapegoating was performed to transfer the guilt of the people to the ritual animal, so society repeatedly identifies victims who function as scapegoats to relieve societal stress. Whether one should go so far as to argue that all religion originates with acts of sacred violence (as does Girard himself), it is imperative for us to critically examine how readily and with what motivation we turn to violence in order to resolve conflict.

If, as Girard argues, the cross of Jesus reveals the power of the scapegoat mechanism, then Christians bear a responsibility to examine and criticize all other acts of violence insofar as they too mask the dynamics of scapegoating. One meaning of Jesus' death is that by this means "God was pleased to reconcile to himself all things, whether on earth or in heaven, by making peace through the blood of his cross" (Col 1:20). Christ died that violence might cease and reconciliation prevail.

This means Christians continue to see as part of their mission the relief of suffering for victims of violence—whether in domestic situations, local communities, or international conflicts. But it means furthermore that Christians advocate legislation that establishes just relations as the basis for peace. As has been said many times before, those who seek peace must work for justice. Where conflict threatens, Christians must prophetically call into question premature attempts to resort to violence, scrutinizing the situation according to the scapegoat phenomenon and insisting on negotiation as the better course. It is in the public arena that Christians are challenged to realize the injunction: "Go in peace; serve the Lord."

The three priorities for social ministry cited in this chapter by no means exhaust the list of topics requiring faithful response by Christians. Other priorities also summon forth serious attention: racism, sexism, and human rights, to name but three others. A strong case can be made for congregations to address as many of these themes as possible. As a matter of fact, these additional issues intersect at many points with the subjects dealt with in this chapter. Concern for God's creation, the hungry, and peace, however, are among those imperatives that belong on every congregation's social ministry agenda. The vision of God's *shalom* summons us to action.

CONGREGATIONAL PRAXIS

To provide congregational leadership for social ministry requires a carefully considered and wise strategy. Opinions will vary greatly whether congregations ought to get involved at all, let alone the question of which course of action should be followed. One who leads in the area of social ministry, particularly in advocacy efforts, must have a strong relationship of trust established with those members who will disagree. If the congregation is to serve as a community of moral deliberation, the commitment to mutual concern for one another must be presupposed which any disagreement about controversial issues does not destroy. This is not to argue that controversy should be avoided. Indeed, some of the best courses of action are only discovered through the give and take of conflicting opinions. But it is to say that a leader must measure the urgency of the social issue over against the ability of the congregation to sustain discord.

Leaders of congregations have the responsibility of listening carefully to members of the congregation to hear reservations they have regarding social advocacy in general as well as the objections they have against a particular position. On the basis of such careful listening, leaders must next discern the cutting edge of the congregation in proposing a particular type of involvement in social ministry. To operate at the "cutting edge" means to encourage a particular social ministry response that challenges members to an ever deeper level of engagement without provoking an exaggerated reaction against such involvement. A leader must take pains in the process of discernment to ascertain just where this "edge" might be. One seeks to lead at that edge, neither lagging behind the consensus of the congregation nor leading too far out in front of the pack.

Leadership in social ministry involves examining the budget of a congregation for its commitment to benevolence. One of the key indicators of a congregation's mission consciousness is the percentage of offerings given toward the common ministry of the denomination and other benevolent causes. A congregation that is ready to direct a significant portion of its offerings toward local, regional, and global social ministry demonstrates that it understands that the congregation does not exist to be served but to serve the cause of the Christ who gave his life for the sake of others. Every congregation needs to be continually vigilant in examining its budgetary priorities.

In selecting which social ministry projects to undertake, several factors deserve consideration. First, one must measure the gifts, abilities, and energy level of congregation members. One must make sure that the congregation has the capacity to complete the projects to which it commits. Second, one must analyze community and global needs to discover which problems cry out for redress. Such needs must be prioritized because the number of possible involvements is infinite. Those needs initially identified on the basis of first impression may prove on closer examination not to be the most appropriate objects of a congregation's involvement. Third, one must devise an approach that does not rob the "recipients" of either their dignity or their ability to act for themselves. Fourth, one should devise projects that have a manageable scope, so that there is clear focus on what can and cannot be reasonably accomplished. Fifth, long-term projects must include a strategy for continually involving new people in carrying out the work.

A congregational consensus will almost always be easier to attain in matters dealing with social service rather than those that deal with social advocacy. Congregations can build upon an established consensus regarding social service in developing an understanding of the issues that require social advocacy. As one learns more about those who suffer as victims in need of Christian charity, one eventually is confronted with the question of how to more effectively change the circumstances under which people become victims in the first place. The link between social service and social advocacy is inexorable, yet necessitates conscientious efforts at education in order to become transparent.

Where a congregational leader seeks a greater degree of engagement in social ministry than a particular congregation seems able to provide, or where one becomes frustrated by a congregation's inability to move into deeper involvement in social ministry, energy can be channeled into ecumenical or secular advocacy organizations where a common cause can be shared with others who share a similar vision. Organizations like Bread for the World, Amnesty International, Sierra Club, or the Fellowship of Reconciliation offer opportunities for involvement in creative social transformation, often assisting in locating those who share a common concern within a geographical area. As one becomes active in such a group, one is wise to have conversation with members of the congregation about the distinction between one's personal involvement as a citizen and one's role as a representative of the congregation per se.

As we conclude this discussion of congregational social ministry, it is important to reiterate that social ministry is one of eight components in the model developed in this book. Its importance should neither be overemphasized nor underemphasized as a vital dimension of congregational life. One particular danger with regard to social ministry is that its proper place be distorted. While the ministry of a congregation is impoverished where social service and social advocacy are insufficiently developed, so too the entire ministry of a congregation cannot be reduced to social ministry. To discern and maintain proper balance in congregational social ministry is a perpetual task. But the stakes are too high not to undertake the challenge.

FOR FURTHER READING

Barndt, Joseph. *Dismantling Racism: The Continuing Challenge to White America.* Minneapolis: Augsburg, 1991.

Birch, Bruce C., and Rasmussen, Larry L. *Bible and Ethics in Christian Life.* Minneapolis: Augsburg, 1989.

Folk, Jerry. *Doing Theology, Doing Justice.* Minneapolis: Fortress, 1991.

Holland, Joe, and Henriot, Peter, S. J. *Social Analysis: Linking Faith and Justice.* Maryknoll: Orbis, 1986.

Kysar, Robert. *Called to Care: Biblical Images for Social Ministry.* Minneapolis: Fortress, 1991.

Maguire, Daniel C. *The Moral Core of Judaism and Christianity: Reclaiming the Revolution.* Minneapolis: Fortress, 1993.

Mauser, Ulrich. *Gospel of Peace: A Scriptural Message for Today's World.* Louisville: Westminster/John Knox, 1992.

Nessan, Craig L. "Stopping Hunger: A Matter of *Status Confessionis?" Lutheran Partners* 13 (May/June 1997): 33–37.

Sider, Ronald J. *Rich Christians in an Age of Hunger.* Dallas: Word, 1990.

Simon, Arthur. *Bread for the World.* New York: Paulist, 1975.

CONCLUSION

"ONE LONG EPICLESIS"

Congregations receive vigor from the Spirit of God, who in-spires them through worship. The "theology of the congregation" developed in the preceding chapters gains its breath in the regular con-spiring of the baptized in Sunday worship. In each of the eight chapters dealing with various facets of congregational life, connections with worship and liturgy have been made explicit. The reader is encouraged to employ creative imagination to continue this work of trans-spiring worship themes into congregational praxis.

The kingdom of God, which we pretend at worship, must extend into the liturgy of daily life. God's Spirit intends more than ritual performance, as crucial as that might be for the sake of our conversion. The Spirit of God wills the transformation of our very lives and our world according to kingdom impulses. The movement from sanctuary to streets and back again thus defines the very rhythm of congregational existence.

The model of congregational life proposed in this book revolves around two foci: (1) that which serves the formation and preservation of Christian *identity* and (2) that which directs the congregation into the world in *mission*. In a sense, these two are reverse sides of a single coin. A church that knows its true identity does mission. A church engaged in mission acts out its fundamental identity.

Yet in institutional practice, the two, identity and mission, often become disjointed. Just as the relationships between faith and works, justification and justice, or the second and third articles of the creed tend to become severed, so congregations are tempted to dissect in practice what ought to be held together. It is for heuristic purposes that the two foci are here distinguished. If the model achieves its intended purpose, however, both will be maintained as indispensable and inseparable constituents of congregational life.

The theology of the congregation here presented is designed to assist congregational leaders, lay and ordained, to examine the theology and practice in their own contexts. The model is intended to function as a mirror by which to reflect upon the dynamics in one's own congregation. Please recall the critical leadership skill of listening, taking the time to pay attention to one's own context prior to advocating change. The various dimensions of congregational life examined in this model are likely already present in varied manifestations, though perhaps in attenuated forms.

Although each context is unique, the central foci of identity and mission deserve nurture in every congregation. Therefore, the components serving identity (worship, education, fellowship, and stewardship) and those serving mission (evangelism, global connections, ecumenism, and social ministry) are proposed as essential dimensions of every congregation's life. The scale at which larger congregations can address each of these components will naturally be different from the scale attainable among smaller ones. Nonetheless, each congregation can direct some attention to each of these eight components. To the degree to which any component is absent, one suspects a diminishment of congregational vitality.

The eight components of this model live in dynamic interrelationship one with another. While worship has been allotted prominence, all eight should be understood to inform each other mutually. For example, fellowship understood as "friendship with the crucified" leads congregation members into organizing acts of social ministry on behalf of the least of Jesus' sisters and brothers. Or developing global connections with distant members of Christ's church serves to further our education about the nature of Christ's body in the world. By no means should these eight components be understood as fixed and isolated categories. Creative congregational programs link them together in new and exciting combinations.

Congregational leaders are challenged to examine ministry in their local context according to the foci and components of this model. Over the course of a congregation's history, it will be important at certain junctures to emphasize one focus or component over others, to compensate for and balance potential distortions. A congregation that has suffered major conflict, on the one hand, may need to concentrate on rebuilding identity before intentionally focusing on mission. A lethargic congregation, on the other hand, may urgently need to recover its calling to do evangelism or social ministry. Leaders must be wise in their discernment regarding which areas require chief attention at a given moment in a congregation's history. Articulating one's own theological model for the congregation can assist greatly in analyzing present practice and inviting others into dialogue about future direction.

One potential caveat for this approach: it may leave the impression that congregational ministry is an end in itself. There is a serious danger of overvaluing what Christians do within and explicitly for their congregations. Conversely, leaders of congregations often appear to undervalue the service to the neighbor implicitly offered in the course of everyday life. Those who spend a lot of time at church meetings are considered "better" members than those who are "too busy" with their jobs. It would be a mistake to think about the ministry of the Christian congregation and its members according to such reasoning.

While this book aims to encourage faithful thinking about the theology undergirding congregational life, the ultimate reason for the organization of congregations is sacrificial service to God and neighbor. By virtue of baptism, God in Christ has made a claim on the totality of our lives. Christians must comprehend that the service rendered in daily life, what is done in many and varied daily vocations (at home, school, and work), is no less service of God than that which takes place within the walls of a church building. The false dichotomy between what one does as a member of a congregation and what one does as a baptized child of God in the world must be overcome. Only then will we begin to realize the expansive vision of Luther's "priesthood of all believers."

We live, like generations before us, at a time when congregations are tested and tempted from every side. Some would argue that in this post-Christian age, it is doubtful the congregation can survive as a viable institution. Indeed, increasing financial pressures threaten the survival of many congregations, forcing them to reconfigure or perish. A prevailing apocalyptic mood threatens to turn congregations inward upon themselves. Quick fixes that promise "church growth" appear to deliver results in a few situations, but may really sell out the gospel in the process of attempting artificial re-spiration.

Clearly, congregations, as expressions of the church, can become perfunctory, routinized, hollow shells. In every time and place, the Christian congregation constantly requires what Yves Congar calls "one long epiclesis," that is, the continual invocation of the living Spirit of the living God to breathe life into its forms. One crucial task of leaders is to prayerfully invoke the spirit of Christ to enliven all we intend to be and do as congregations. Without the invocation of the living Spirit of God, every model of congregational life and all theology of the congregation remain dead bones. Can these bones be made to live (Ez 37:1-14)?

Come, Holy Spirit!

NAME INDEX

SCRIPTURE INDEX

SUBJECT INDEX

99837

kerygma, 3f., 43

kingdom of God, 4, 21, 22, 24-27, 28, 35, 37-40, 42, 59, 66, 71, 81, 96, 114, 117, 124

koinonia, 4f., 32

law, 62, 68f., 115

leaders/leadership, 8, 20, 22, 121, 124-127

liturgy, 10-12, 37-44, 51, 53, 54, 56, 59, 69, 85-89, 96f.

love, 13, 31, 42, 56, 59, 71, 73-77

mission, viif., 7, 9, 22, 32, 40f., 44, 46, 50, 55, 73, 77, 80f., 91-93, 97f., 104, 111, 124-27

model, 7, 11, 124f.

money, 72f., 113, 121

nationalism, 90, 94-96

offering, 38, 68

ownership, 68-71

parenesis, 29-32, 41

pastor, 61-66

peace, 39, 41, 43, 99, 112, 115, 119f.

persecution, 3, 47, 91

poor, 16f, 18f

post-Christian, 16, 46, 55, 126

prayer, 38, 43, 49, 59, 60, 63, 66, 74, 88, 97, 101, 106

pretending, 34-37, 59

priesthood of all believers, 45, 54, 126

race, 44, 59, 90, 91, 93, 94, 98, 120

reconciliation, 6, 31, 102, 104

resurrection, 26, 113

ritual, 34, 35, 36, 48

sacraments, 28, 29, 40, 88, 101

saints, 45, 50, 51-53, 55, 60

salvation, 80f., 88, 116, 117, 120

Scripture, 3, 10, 19, 20-22, 30, 38, 42, 45, 49, 54, 63, 65, 88, 92, 96, 102f.

sin, 21, 30, 37, 50, 53, 60, 61

small catechism, 28

social ministry, 43, 81, 108-11

spiritual gifts, 59, 60, 64

state, 46, 94-96, 112

tithing, 68, 71-73, 77

violence, 76, 95f., 97, 99, 119f.

visiting, 14, 83f.

wealth, 26, 71, 94

Word and Sacrament, 24, 28, 32, 40, 51, 61, 74, 86, 87, 88

workplace, 19f., 75, 126

worship, viii, 7, 8, 10f., 14, 29, 75, 82, 85-86, 97, 107f., 117-120, 124

youth, 47f., 49, 50, 51, 53, 54, 60, 64-66

3 4711 00153 7721